First-Rate Reading™ ^Basics

Phonemic Awareness & Phonics

Grades 2-3

by Starin W. Lewis

Carson-Dellosa Publishing Company, Inc. • Greensboro, North Carolina

Credits and Dedication

Project Director:

Kelly Gunzenhauser

Layout Design:

Jon Nawrocik

Inside Illustrations:

Stefano Giorgi

Cover Design:

Peggy Jackson

Cover Illustrations:

Stefano Giorgi

This book is dedicated to my former teachers, from preschool to graduate school. Without you, I would not have my love for learning. Thank you for all of your long hours, your enthusiasm, and your commitment to this field.

-S. L.

Table of Contents

Introduction

Phonemic awareness and phonics are different; phonemic awareness instruction teaches children the sounds (or phonemes) in words, while phonics instruction teaches the written representations (graphemes) of those sounds. Both forms of instruction are necessary to teach most students how to read. Phonemic awareness skills include sound identification, manipulation, and substitution. Here is a brief definition of each phonemic awareness skill taught in this book:

- Phoneme Awareness Review—a look back at skills students should already be developing, such as identifying individual sounds and determining whether they are the same or different
- Phoneme Blending—blending individual sounds to make words
- Phoneme Segmentation—counting the number of sounds in words
- Phoneme Manipulation—deleting, adding, and substituting different sounds in words
- Basic Syllabication—counting the number of sound "chunks" in words

After students understand phonemic awareness, they learn that letters represent phonemes. Here is a brief definition of each phonics skill taught in this book:

- Long Vowels—identifying how to use letter combinations to make vowels "say their names"
- Digraphs—combinations that make single sounds, such as *ph*, *ea*, or *th*
- Variant Vowels—vowel/letter combinations that make neither long nor short vowel sounds, such as any vowel + *r* combination
- Diphthongs—any vowel combination in which pronunciation begins similarly to one recognized vowel sound and as spoken, moves to another, as the /*oy*/ sound in *toy*

Send home the reproducible Parent Letter (page 5) to reinforce phonics and phonemic awareness instruction at home. The more parents read and work with letters with their children, the more ready for further instruction their children will be.

Finally, use the Assessments (pages 6-7) to look at students' phonemic awareness and phonics levels at any time during the school year, including before instruction begins. Assessing students early in the year will help you determine areas in which they need practice. It will also help you group students by skill level, even if your preference is to group students with a range of skills. The first page of this two-page assessment tests students on phonemic awareness, and the second page assesses phonics. Depending on where students are in their reading development, you may choose to give students both assessments at once, or give them the phonemic awareness assessment at the beginning of the year and wait to assess phonics when students have reviewed some skills in both areas.

Parent Letter

Dear Parents/Family:

Research shows that good readers are more successful in school. Reading is used in all other subjects and is critical for success in real life. It is important for your child to develop a solid reading base of phonemic awareness (sounds in words) and phonics (understanding letters that make those sounds). Following are suggestions and information about this area of instruction.

Phonemic Awareness is the ability to work with individual sounds and to hear syllables. This understanding should precede working with printed text. Help your child improve in phonemic awareness by doing the following:

- Make up and analyze rhymes. Say a word, such as *dog*, and ask your child to name words that rhyme (*log, fog, hog, frog*). Then, ask your child to name which sound in the word *dog* changes (/d/).
- Clap syllables in your child's name. For example, if your child's name is Jordan, clap once for *Jor* and once for *dan*. Teach your child how to clap other words.
- Help your child blend and separate sounds. Say the word *cat* and have her identify the three sounds (/k/, short /a/, /t/) in the word. Then, say the three sounds separately and have her blend them together to make a word.

Phonics skills require students to understand that the letters in the alphabet represent all of the sounds they make when speaking or reading. Help your child improve in phonics by doing the following:

- Review the alphabet. Give your child a long word and ask him to make as many smaller words as he can. Or, move from simple alphabet books to more "grown-up" versions, such as *The Z Was Zapped* by Chris Van Allsburg (Houghton Mifflin, 1987).
- Work with your child on spelling simple words using both sound-spelling techniques (spell it like it sounds) and familiar spelling patterns (c-a-r-t = cart, so s-m-a-r-t = ?).

Using these ideas will help your child begin to enjoy reading. For more information, please feel free to contact me.

Sincerely,

_____

Name _____   *Assessment*

Date _____

Phonemic Awareness

I. Phoneme Identity: Total ___/6
Say the following words. Have the student identify the same sound in the words.
1. tip, tan, tub (/t/)
2. mix, mug, mad (/m/)
3. bell, mail, tool (/l/)
4. cup, lap, sip (/p/)
5. dot, mop, rock (short /o/)
6. big, sip, chin (short /i/)

II. Phoneme Categorization: Total ___/6
Say the following words. Have the student name the word with a different beginning sound.
1. lake, leaf, jog (jog)
2. hid, goat, give (hid)
3. bird, cat, bake (cat)
4. side, boat, seed (boat)
5. lip, wag, weed (lip)
6. dog, yard, yes (dog)

III. Phoneme Blending: Total ___/6
Say each sound separately. Ask the student to blend the sounds to form a word.
1. /r/, long /o/, /b/ (robe)
2. /n/, short /e/, /s/, /t/ (nest)
3. /p/, long /a/, /j/ (page)
4. /l/, long /i/, /t/ (light)
5. /h/, short /a/, /m/ (ham)
6. /d/, short /u/, /k/ (duck)

IV. Phoneme Segmentation: Total ___/6
Say the following words. Have the student count the number of sounds in each word.
1. bag (3)
2. fast (4)
3. goat (3)
4. each (2)
5. lift (4)
6. sheet (3)

V. Syllabication: Total ___/6
Say the following words. Ask the student to count the syllables in each word.
1. addition (3)
2. award (2)
3. sunshine (2)
4. unfriendly (3)
5. rainbow (2)
6. thermometer (4)

VI. Phoneme Manipulation: Total ___/6
Say the following words. Ask the student to take off the beginning sound and substitute the new sound in parentheses.
1. mop (/h/) (hop)
2. jump (/b/) (bump)
3. dime (/t/) (time)
4. clash (/s/) (slash)
5. dress (/p/) (press)
6. block (/k/) (clock)

First-Rate Reading™: Phonemic Awareness and Phonics • CD-104019 • © Carson-Dellosa
Basics

Phonics

I. Long Vowel Sounds: Total ___/6

Write the following words on index cards. Have the student read each word. Write the word the student says.

1. time _____   2. neat _____   3. play _____

4. hold _____   5. light _____   6. grow _____

II. Digraphs: Total ___/6

Write the following words on index cards. Have the student read each word. Write the word the student says.

1. shell_____   2. hen_____   3. chip _____

4. ring _____   5. knit _____   6. phase_____

III. Variant Vowels: Total ___/6

Write the following words on index cards. Have the student read each word. Write the word the student says.

1. dirt_____   2. fare_____   3. jar _____

4. law _____   5. pale _____   6. corn _____

IV. Diphthongs: Total ___/6

Write the following words on index cards. Have the student read each word. Write the word the student says.

1. coin_____   2. soil _____   3. toy _____

4. loud _____   5. out _____   6. down _____

Phonemic Awareness

Introduction: Phoneme Identity, Categorization, and Blending

By second grade, students should have some familiarity with basic phonemic awareness concepts, even if some students have not mastered these skills. Use these activities as a warm-up for further phonemic awareness work and to assess which students may need extra help.

Student ID

Remind students that words are made up of sounds. Say the word *pancake* and ask them to identify the beginning sound (/p/). Say three words that have one sound in common, such as *toy, tall,* and *tack.* Ask, "What sound is the same in all three words?" Students should identify the /t/ sound at the beginning of each word. If necessary, give students more practice with additional words. Challenge students to brainstorm their own words in groups. Divide the class into groups of three. Direct each group to quietly brainstorm and write down three words that have the same beginning sound. Check each group's words to make sure there is only one duplicate sound, then have one group come to the front of the classroom. Let each group member say one of the words as the rest of the class tries to identify the common sound. Ask the group if the class is correct. Repeat with the remaining groups.

All Aboard the Ending Sound Train

Reinforce the concept of ending sounds with picture references. Explain that words are made up of sounds. These sounds can come at the beginning, middle, or end of a word. For example, ask, "What sound do you hear at the end of the word *cat?*" Then, ask, "What sound is the same in the words *sun, bin,* and *can?*" Students should identify the /t/ and /n/ sounds. Give students more practice if they have difficulty identifying the ending sounds. Next, give each student three white paper squares, each approximately 3" x 3" (7.5 cm x 7.5 cm), a piece of black paper, string, scissors, crayons or markers, and access to a hole punch. Direct each student to think of three objects that have the same ending sound and that are easy to draw. For example, drawing a *bus* is much easier than drawing the word *pass.* Have each student draw her three objects on the three white paper squares (train cars), then punch a hole on the right side of one drawing, on the left and right sides of the second drawing, and on the left side of the third drawing. Have each student cut two pieces of string and tie the train cars together. Let each child create an engine with the black paper and attach it to the front of the train. Allow students to show their projects to the class. Have the class identify the ending sound that is the same in all three pictures. Post the trains around the classroom. For an extra challenge, have students try to identify train cars that show words with the same beginning sounds.

Class Sound Identification Book

Ask students to identify the same sound in the following word sets: *moon, mitt, mask* (/m/); *kid, bud, mad* (/d/); and *pan, cat, mad* (short /a/). Give students paper and crayons. Challenge each student to think of three objects (or more) that have the same sound. Tell students that the same sound can be at the beginning, middle, or end of a word. Have each student draw all three objects on the same page and write the names of the objects. Also, have students add decorative borders to the pages. Assemble the pages into a class book. As you share the book with the class, ask the author of each page to identify the three objects on his page. Direct the rest of the class to identify which sound is the same.

No Match

Explain that some signs have a special symbol on them that means *no*. It is a circle with a diagonal slash through the middle, and it is usually red. For example, a No Pets Allowed sign could be represented by a picture of dog with a red circle and slash over it. Draw an example of the symbol on the board. Give each student a red chenille craft stick. Direct students to bend part of the craft stick into a circle, and twist the leftover end piece to go diagonally across the middle of the circle to make the No symbol. Say three words: two words with the same beginning sound and one word with a different beginning sound. For example, say "table, couch, tire." As you repeat the words, have students raise their No symbols when they hear the word that does not match the other words (*couch*). Let students suggest other word groups.

Sound Sort Show-and-Tell

Send a note home asking for each student to bring in a random object from home. Explain that any object a student can carry will work, except for anything living, perishable, or very messy. Designate a show-and-tell day for students to show off their objects. Let each student come to the front of the classroom and describe her object without saying the name of the object. Let a volunteer name the object and isolate the beginning sound. For example, if a student brings in a toy dog, the volunteer should raise his hand and then say, "dog, /d/." The student who brings in the dog is now the keeper of the /d/ sound. Have her sit down and keep the dog on her desk. Any other student who brings in an object that starts with the /d/ sound should place his object on her desk next to the dog. Continue until all objects have been sorted. Then, call on volunteers who do not have a lot of objects to redistribute the objects. Allow a volunteer to go to the /d/ pile and name each object as she returns it to its owner. Tally the objects in each group to determine which group was the largest.

Find It First, Fast!

Use this speed game to help students identify beginning sounds more quickly. Specify a sound for students, such as /p/. When you say, "Go," have students walk around the classroom to find things that begin with that sound. Tell students that they should find things as quickly as possible without running. The last student to find an object must sit down, but she may choose the next beginning sound. A beginning sound may be called more than once, but each student must find a different object from the one she found before. Continue until only one student is standing. Let that student begin the next game or post her name on the board for the day. Repeat until students can automatically identify objects that match beginning sounds.

Counters and Cups

Give each student a small, plastic cup and three plastic counters or pennies. Have each student place the three counters in a row in front of him. Explain that you will say three words, and each word is represented by a counter. When each student hears the word that has a different beginning sound, he should place a cup over the corresponding counter. For example, if you say the words *hair*, *hat*, and

potato, explain that the first counter represents the first word (*hair*), the second counter represents the second word (*hat*), and the third counter represents the third word (*potato*). Repeat the three words and direct each student to place a cup over the counter that represents the different word (*potato*). Repeat with additional word groups.

Find a Friend

Say three words—two that begin with the same sound and one that begins with a different sound, such as *car*, *kite*, and *lunch*. Ask, "Which word contains the odd sound?" Students should identify the word *lunch*. Then, tell students, "Let's think of a friend (matching word) for the odd word so that *lunch* isn't alone anymore. What is another word that has the same beginning sound as *lunch*?" After students find a "friend" for *lunch*, repeat with other word groups. Also repeat with middle sounds and ending sounds. Then, allow each student to walk around and find a friend that has a matching sound in her name. For example, Lily may find Logan because both students' names start with the /l/ sound. Rasheed and Dean may pair up for middle sounds, and Trina and Isabella may pair up for ending sounds. Tell students that they may find more than one friend at a time, as long as all students in each group have the matching sound in the same places in their names. Find a friend for yourself each time, as well.

Phoneme Blending

Introduction

Blending phonemes involves saying individual sounds closely together so that those sounds combine to make words. Students should have a good idea about how to blend individual sounds, but even skilled students benefit from practicing this skill with more difficult words.

Blending Review

Remind students that the smallest sounds in language are called *phonemes*. When students blend those sounds together, the sounds make words. Give students an example by saying three individual sounds, such as /t/, short /o/, and /p/. Ask students to identify the word *top*. Give students more practice by saying each set of sounds from the first word list below and having them blend the sounds into a word. When you have said the first word list, explain that some words have digraphs. A *digraph* is two letters together that make one sound (*ch*, *sh*, *th*, *ph*, *ea*, etc.). Guide students to blend words with digraphs using the Digraph Word List below. Later the same day or sometime the next day, randomly say words from both lists and have students identify the words with digraphs.

Word List	Digraph Word List
can (/k/, short /a/, /n/)	thin (/th/, short /i/, /n/)
leaf (/l/, long /e/, /f/)	shape (/sh/, long /a/, /p/)
must (/m/, short /u/, /s/, /t/)	cheese (/ch/, long /e/, /z/)
crisp (/k/, /r/, short /i/, /s/, /p/)	shelf (/sh/, short /e/, /l/, /f/)
spot (/s/, /p/, short /o/, /t/)	ranch (/r/, short /a/, /n/, /ch/)

Blend That Word!

Write the words below on index cards. Write the corresponding phoneme numbers on the backs of the cards. (Adjust numbers to match regional pronunciations.) Tape the cards to the board, number side up. Assign students to two teams. Explain that the numbers on the index cards show the number of sounds in the words. The higher the number, the longer the word and the more points to be earned. Have a student from Team A select a number between two and five. Pick a card with that number and say each phoneme to his team. Let team members work together to blend the sounds, then have the student who chose the number say the blended word. If he blends the word correctly, write the corresponding number of points on the board and let Team B have a turn. If the team blends the word incorrectly, they get no points, and Team B may try. Alternate until there are no cards left. The team with the most points at the end of the game wins.

2—if (short /i/, /f/)   3—boat (/b/, long /o/, /t/)
2—he (/h/, long /e/)   3—time (/t/, long /i/, /m/)
2—am (short /a/, /m/)   3—duck (/d/, short /u/, /k/)
4—fast (/f/, short /a/, /s/, /t/)
4—stop (/s/, /t/, short /o/, /p/)
4—lunch (/l/, short /u/, /n/, /ch/)
5—window (/w/, short /i/, /n/, /d/, long /o/)
5—spend (/s/, /p/, short /e/, /n/, /d/)
5—zebra (/z/, long /e/, /b/, /r/, short /u/)

Climb the Ladder

Remind students that words are made of sounds. There are words that have two sounds, such as *he*, words that have three sounds, such as *wave*, words that have four sounds, such as *fast*, etc. Have students play Climb the Ladder, a blending sounds game. Assign students to teams of five. Direct each team to line up facing you to make the rungs on a "ladder." Choose a team to go first, then say two individual sounds to the first "rung" (student) in line. (See list below for suggested words.) Ask the student to blend the sounds to form a word. If the student gets it right, write one point on the board for her team. If the student gets it wrong, the team gets no points. Have the first student remain in line and sit down, and move to the next line. After the first student in each line has had a chance to blend a two-phoneme word, begin a new round by saying three-phoneme words to the second students in line. Again, give each team one point for each correctly blended word. Repeat with four-, five-, and six-phoneme words. The line with the most points wins the game.

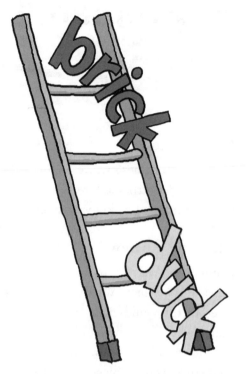

Suggested Words:

Two phonemes—if, be, day, my, go, at

Three phonemes—jet, lip, hop, duck, cat, bike

Four phonemes—flame, sweet, slide, graph, brick, west

Five phonemes—music, pupil, splash, August, asleep, winter

Six phonemes—basket, sprint, snowman, notebook, sunshine, backpack

Blender

Have student pairs play Blender. Give each pair three minutes to think of a two-phoneme word, such as *if*, and divide the sounds so that each student has a sound. For example, one student would say the short /i/ and the other student would say the /f/. Select a pair to say their sounds and have the rest of the class blend the sounds to form the word. Continue until all pairs have a chance to say their sounds. Next, say, "Blender," and have students move around the room as if they are being whirled around in a blender. Say, "Off" or turn the lights off and on as a signal for students to stop moving around and quickly form groups of three. This time, challenge each group to think of a three-phoneme word and assign a sound for each student in the group to say. Call on each group to say their sounds to the class. Have the rest of the class blend the sounds to form a three-phoneme word. Say, "Blender!" one more time. Have students move around and form four-student groups, and continue the game with four-phoneme words. To extend play, call random numbers for students to use to find groups and choose words, or continue to increase the number of group members and phonemes.

First-Rate Reading™: Phonemic Awareness and Phonics • CD-104019 • © Carson-Dellosa
Basics

Tying Sounds Together

Write each of the following letter sounds on an index card: short /a/, /b/, /k/, /d/, short /e/, /f/, /g/, /h/, short /i/, /j/, /l/, /m/, /n/, short /o/, /p/, /r/, /s/, /t/, short /u/, /v/, /w/, /ch/, /sh/, /th/, long /a/, long /e/, long /i/, long /o/, long /u/. Provide a ball of yarn for this activity. Assign one sound to each student. Remind students that when they "tie" sounds together, they form words. For example, if they tie the sounds /h/, short /o/, and /p/ together, they get the word *hop*. Have students sit in a circle and hold up their letter sound cards. Hand one end of the yarn to the student holding the /b/ card. Pass the rest of the yarn ball to the student holding the short /u/. Have that student hold the strand of yarn and hand the rest of the ball to the student holding the /s/. Say, "Tie these sounds together to form a word." Have each student holding the yarn say her letter sound (/b/, short /u/, /s/). Ask the rest of the class to blend the three sounds to form the word *bus*. Retrieve the yarn and choose additional words to use to repeat the exercise, such as *fun, mop, bell, gift, kept, ran, wake, teeth, shut, chip, nag, home, vest, time,* and *cube.* (Warn students that since they are practicing letter sounds, the correct spellings of the words may use different letters.) After several examples, have students think of their own words. Select a student to hand out the yarn ball and direct the rest of the class to blend the sounds.

Sound Play

Assign students to pairs. Give each pair a copy of the Sound Play reproducible (page 14) on heavy paper. Have students cut apart the cards, then combine pairs to form groups of four students. Explain that each pair is still a team. Give each group a piece of paper and a pencil. Have each team place their cards facedown in front of them. Instruct Player 1 on Team A to take a card and read the word to himself, think about how to break the word into sounds, then say each sound to his partner, Player 2. For example, if the word on the card is *best*, Player 1 should say the sounds /b/, short /e/, /s/, and /t/. Player 2 should then blend the sounds to form the word. If Player 2 is correct, the group members should record one point for Team A on the paper, and it is Team B's turn. After Team B takes their turn, have Team A go again and let the partners switch roles. The student who read before should now blend the sounds. When all of the cards have been used, the team with the most points wins the game.

Sound Play

Cut apart the cards. Use
them with the game called Sound Play.

flat	stem
list	crop
plum	log
nest	swim
past	dug

Phoneme Segmenting

Introduction

Segmenting, the opposite of blending, is a skill that requires students to listen to a word and separate it into its individual sounds. Students who have practiced blending may have more difficulty with segmenting and vice versa, but generally, practice in one skill improves skill levels in the other.

Word Ripping

Remind students that words are made of individual sounds. For example, the word *sock* has three sounds: /s/, short /o/, and /k/. Explain that saying individual sounds is almost like breaking a word apart. Model this concept for students using long strips of paper. Repeat the word *sock* while holding a strip of paper. Tear off a piece of paper as you say each sound. Ask, "How many sounds are in the word *sock*? There are three. You can tell because we have three pieces of paper torn off." Guide students in practicing the same concept. Give each student two strips of paper. Say a word from the word list below and have students repeat it, then break it into individual sounds. As each student says each sound, have him tear off a piece of paper. When students have torn off the correct number of pieces of paper, ask, "How many sounds are in that word?"

Suggested words and number of phonemes:

rice (3)	vote (3)
tail (3)	feast (4)
she (2)	play (3)
throat (4)	scratch (5)

Phoneme Count

Use the Phoneme Count game to reinforce the concept that words are made of individual sounds. Ask, "How many sounds are there in the word *bread*?" Write *bread* on the board and add the number 4. Explain that there are five letters in the word, but only four sounds. Give students more practice counting sounds if necessary. Then, assign students to groups of two, three, or four, and give each member in a group a different colored game piece, such as a math manipulative. Give each group one copy of the Phoneme Count Cards reproducible and the Phoneme Count Board reproducible (pages 16-17) for every game you plan to play. Tell students to cut apart the cards on the Phoneme Count Cards reproducible. Direct students to place the cards facedown, mix them up, and place them in a pile. Have each student place his game piece on the "start" space on his group's Phoneme Count Board. Have Player A move first. Tell Player B to pick a card from the deck and read the word to Player A. Player A should then count and say the number of sounds in the word. If Player A is correct, have her move the same amount of spaces as there are sounds in the word. Then, it is Player B's turn, and Player C reads the card. Play continues until one player reaches the end. (Players do not need an exact number of sounds to reach the end.)

Phoneme Count Cards

Cut apart the cards and use
them with the Phoneme Count game.

dog (3)	kick (3)	left (4)	no (2)
sweep (4)	brake (4)	why (2)	cone (3)
stamp (5)	chip (3)	club (4)	fox (4)
bag (3)	joke (3)	date (3)	stream (5)
five (3)	clap (4)	shelf (4)	block (4)

Phoneme Count Board

Use the game board to play
the Phoneme Count game. Try to get
to the end by counting sounds.

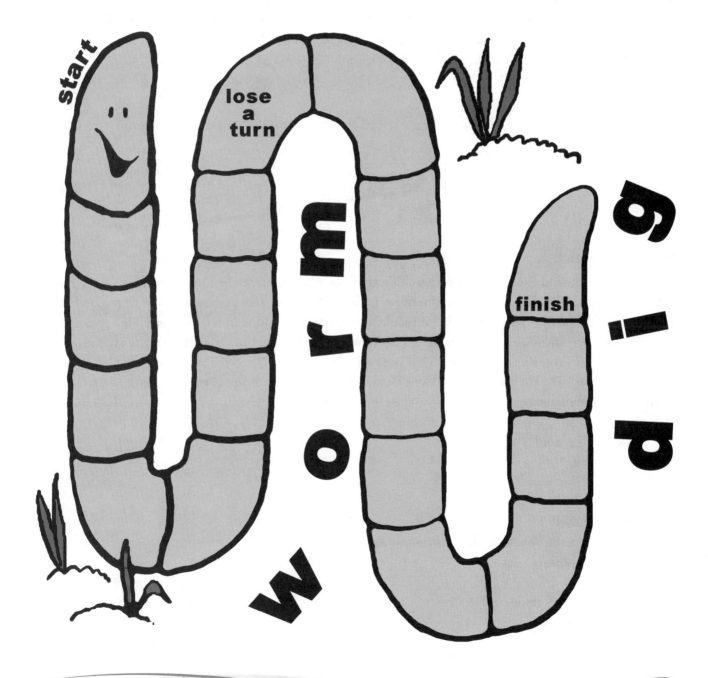

start

lose
a
turn

w o r m

finish

d i g

Sound Break Dancing

Use a kinesthetic activity to have students segment phonemes. Remind students how to break words into individual sounds to do "sound breaks." Explain that there is a form of dance called break dancing. Have students combine the two by performing "sound break dancing." Say a word and have students work independently to break the word into individual sounds. Then, let each student add a dance move while saying each sound. For example, if the word is *top*, a student can say /t/ while turning, short /o/ while taking a step to the side, and /p/ while taking a step back. Let each student make up a move for each sound in the suggested words below. For each word, call on several students to show off their dance (and segmenting) moves. To synchronize moves as a class, let each student create moves for a different word, then have each student teach the class her word. Each word will have a signature move sequence. Suggested words and phonemes*: foot (/f/, /oo/, /t/); house (/h/, /ou/, /s/); much (/m/, short /u/, /ch/); clock (/k/, /l/, short /o/, /k/); again (short /u/, /g/, short /e/, /n/); stamp (/s/, /t/, short /a/, /m/, /p/)

*Adjust number of phonemes to match regional pronunciations.

Sound Sequence

Direct students to stand in a circle and say a word, such as *home*. Choose a student in the circle to say the first sound in the word (/h/). If the student is correct, say nothing. The next student should say the next sound in the word (long /o/). If he is correct, allow the third student to say the next sound in the word (/m/). If a student is incorrect, say "No" and have that student sit down. Allow the next student in the circle to try to say the correct sound. Let students continue until the word has been sounded out. After the word is finished, the next student should say, "Done." The student who says "Done" is also out and must sit down. Continue to give new words until a winner is left standing. Let students who are already seated whisper suggestions for words to you. Following is an example round:

    Teacher: The word is "seven."
    Student 1: /s/
    Student 2: short /e/
    Student 3: /v/
    Student 4: short /a/
    Teacher: No. (Student 4 sits down because of error.)
    Student 5: short /e/
    Student 6: /n/
    Student 7: Done. (Student 7 sits down.)
    Teacher gives new word.

Word Spin Cycle

To prepare, make one copy of the Word Spin Cycle reproducible (page 20). Cut out each spinner. Use a paper fastener to attach a paper clip to the middle of each spinner. Review the process for segmenting words into individual sounds. Assign students to teams of four and have each team choose a team name. Write the names on the board. Explain that the two spinners are different; one spinner has consonants on it and the other has numbers. Spin the letter spinner first, then the number spinner. When you say, "Go," have each team think of a word beginning with the sound that the letter spinner landed on. The word they choose must have the same number of sounds in it as the number that appeared on the number spinner. For example, if the first spin lands on the letter *s* and the second spin lands on the number 3, write *s* and 3 on the board and have each team think of a word that begins with the /s/ sound and has three phonemes, such as *sun, sat, said, sell,* etc. As soon as a team thinks they have found a word that meets the criteria, team members should raise their hands. If they are correct, draw a tally mark under that team's name on the board. If they are incorrect, call on the second team that raises their hands. The team with the most points at the end of the game wins. To extend the activity, have students think of words that have the same ending sound as the letter on the spinner.

Phoneme Bee

Use a spelling bee format to involve the whole class in phoneme segmenting. On the board or on chart paper, create a master list of words to use while playing the game, including words with two, three, four, and five sounds. (For more advanced students, use words with more phonemes.) Write the list in order of easiest words to hardest words and list the number of phonemes next to each word. Call on one student at a time to stand in front of the class. Read a word to that student and ask him to segment the word into its individual sounds. If he is correct, allow him to continue to play. If he is incorrect, he must sit out for the rest of the game. Play until only one student remains and declare her the winner. Reward all students with extra reading time, bee-themed stickers, honey sandwiches, etc. (Get families' permission and check for food allergies and religious or other preferences before providing food.)

Word Spin Cycle

Cut out each circle. Attach
a paper clip to the center of each spinner
with a paper fastener.

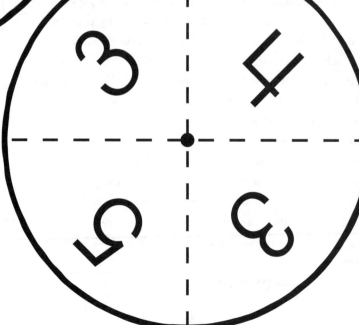

Phoneme Manipulation

Introduction

Phoneme manipulation requires that students be able to delete, add, move, and substitute phonemes in words. This skill leads students to make many new words and form word families using onsets and rimes.

Press the Delete Key

Remind students that words are made up of sounds and explain that these sounds can be added, deleted, moved, or changed. For example, the word *trace* is made up of four individual sounds: /t/, /r/, long /a/, and /s/. Ask, "What would be left if you took off, or deleted, the first sound in *trace*? What is trace without the /t/?" Students should say the word *race*. Have students delete sounds in other words. Give each student a square piece of paper, approximately 1" x 1" (2.5 cm x 2.5 cm). Have each student write the word *delete* on her square. Explain that when you want to erase something on the computer, you press the delete button. Have students tape their "delete keys" to their desks. Ask them to imagine that their desks are computer keyboards. Say some of the following words: *brake (rake), crib (rib), blend (lend), flake (lake), twig (wig), scan (can), snap (nap), spin (pin)*. After each word, direct students to press their "delete keys" to "delete" the first sound in each word. Then, ask students to identify each word without its beginning sound.

Sound Subtraction

Have students work on subtraction problems. Explain that these problems are a little different than math problems because they involve words and sounds. Remind students that words are made up of individual sounds. For example, the word *spot* is made up of four sounds: /s/, /p/, short /o/, and /t/. Ask, "What word is left if you take away the beginning /s/ sound?" Explain that when you "subtract" the /s/ from *spot*, the new word is *pot*. Give students the following sound "subtraction" problems.

1. What is *play* if you take away the /p/? (*lay*)
2. What is *glow* if you take away the /g/? (*low*)
3. What is *pride* if you take away the /p/? (*ride*)
4. What is *stack* if you take away the /s/? (*tack*)
5. What is *stone* if you take away the /s/? (*tone*)
6. What is *swarm* if you take away the /s/? (*warm*)
7. What is *spine* if you take away the /s/? (*pine*)
8. What is *clog* if you take away the /k/? (*log*)

Muting Sounds

Provide a real remote control from home. Remind students that words are made up of individual sounds. For example, the word *twin* is made up of four sounds: /t/, /w/, short /i/, and /n/. Show the remote control to the class. Explain that the mute button turns off the volume. Use the remote to "mute" the first sound in words. Ask, "What word would you have if you muted the first sound in *swing*? In other words, what would *swing* sound like without the beginning /s/ sound?" Students should answer, "wing." Have students mute the first sound in the word *brush*. Tell them to think about what *brush* would sound like without its first sound and raise their hands when they know the answer (*rush*). Point the remote at a student and pretend to click the mute button to take away the beginning sound (but not the rest of the word). The student should say the word without its beginning sound. Continue with other words, such as *craft (raft)*, *drip (rip)*, *cloud (loud)*, *black (lack)*, *smile (mile)*, *score (core)*, and *sport (port)*.

Sound Cover-Up

If students have worked on the previous three activities (Press the Delete Key, Sound Subtraction, and Muting Sounds, pages 21-22), remind students that they have been removing the first sounds in words. Have students work in pairs to remove beginning sounds of words. Give each pair a copy of the Sound Cover-Up reproducible (page 23). Have Partner A cut out the strip of paper. Then, have her cut the slits above and below the word list. (To make cutting slits easier, have each student fold the paper vertically so that the middles of the slits are on the fold, then cut from the middles to the ends of the slits and unfold the paper.) Partner A should weave the strip of paper through the top slit, being careful not to cover any beginning sounds yet. Then, she should read the first word to Partner B. Partner B should try to say the word without its beginning sound. Partner A should check the answer by pulling the strip of paper through the slit so that it covers the first letter of the word. Pairs should continue until the fifth word on the list has been said without its beginning sound. Then, direct partners to switch roles and continue working with the remaining words on the sheet.

Sound Cover-Up

Cut out the strip of paper. Cut the slits. Weave the paper through the slits to cover up the first letters.

1. place
2. flow
3. snail
4. crust
5. proof
6. clock
7. stale
8. drip
9. bring
10. black

Sound Addition

Tell students that they will work on math problems, but they won't be adding and subtracting numbers—they will be adding and subtracting sounds. For example, if students add the /b/ sound to the beginning of the word *lock*, they get the new word *block*. If they add the /f/ sound to the beginning of the word *law*, they will get the new word *flaw*. Give students the sound addition and subtraction problems listed below:

1. What do you get when you add /p/ to *ants*? (*pants*)
2. What do you get when you add /s/ to *lime*? (*slime*)
3. What do you get when you add /k/ to *luck*? (*cluck*)
4. What do you get when you add /f/ to *lake*? (*flake*)
5. What do you get when you add /t/ to *rash*? (*trash*)
6. What do you get when you add /p/ to *rice*? (*price*)
7. What do you get when you subtract /g/ from *grow*? (*row*)
8. What do you get when you subtract /p/ from *grasp*? (*grass*)
9. What do you get when you subtract /s/ from *trace*? (*tray*)
10. What do you get when you subtract /p/ from *sheep*? (*she*)

Magic Sticks

Give each student one craft stick. Explain that when students add sounds to the beginnings of words, they can change words into other words. For example, they can change the word *ray* into *gray* by adding a /g/ sound to the beginning. Have students make "magic sticks" that will help them change words. Give each student a craft stick and assemble art supplies, such as glitter, markers, glue, wiggly eyes, etc. Write the following letter sounds on the board: /b/, /k/, /f/, /g/, /p/, /s/. Direct each student to choose one of these sounds and write it on one side of her craft stick. Then, give students time to decorate their "magic sticks." Next, say, "*lay*." Instruct students to wave their magic sticks and add the sounds on their sticks to the beginning of the word. For example, students with /p/ magic sticks should add /p/ to the beginning of the word to make *play*. Students with a /k/ magic stick should make *clay*. Continue with the words *lap, lad, low, lid, lack*, and *lick*. Explain that each change may make a new word, or it may make a nonsense word. Either is fine; the point is to manipulate sounds. During the activity, call on students with various sounds on their sticks to say their new words to the class.

First-Rate Reading™:Phonemic Awareness and Phonics • CD-104019 • © Carson-Dellosa
Basics

Sound Poets

Remind students that when they add sounds to the beginnings of existing words, sometimes they will make new words. For example, if they add the /s/ sound to the beginning of the word *mile*, they will make the word *smile*. Ask, "What do you notice about the words *mile* and *smile*?" Students should notice that the words rhyme. Challenge each student to make up a short poem using the two words *mile* and *smile*. If the class needs help getting started, give them an example: "After walking *mile* after *mile*, I noticed I had lost my *smile*." Work with students to find other rhymes by adding sounds to the beginnings of different words. Add /p/ to *late* to make *plate*. Then, do the same with /s/ to make *slate*. Have students create poems using a combination of the words *plate*, *slate*, and *late*. Repeat with *lip* and /b/, /f/, /k/, and /s/. Challenge students to come up with poems using all five words—*lip*, *blip*, *flip*, *clip*, and *slip*.

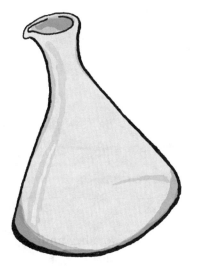

Sound Science

Provide a scientific beaker and test tube for each student, or use one set as an example and let students pretend. Explain that a scientist can create a new compound by adding one chemical to another. Have students be sound scientists. Tell the class that instead of adding chemicals, they will add sounds. Pretend to pour the contents of a test tube into a beaker. Say, "If we take the /s/ sound and add it to the beginning of the word *mall*, we get a whole new word. What would that word be?" Students should answer that the new word is *small*. Next, have students pretend to mix chemicals together as you give them additional sounds and words to combine. Have them try adding /s/ to *tick*, /s/ to *lap*, /p/ to *lump*, /t/ to *weed*, /p/ to *ride*, and /k/ to *rash*.

Building a Family

Use what students are learning to help them build word families using only sounds (not letters). Introduce a common word family ending, such as *-at*. Go around the room and let each student choose a sound to add. For example, if the first student says the word *bat*, ask students if that is a real word. If the next student says the word *zat*, ask if that is a real word. As you call on students, make a list of real words and a list of nonsense words on a piece of paper. When students cannot think of any more sounds to add to *-at*, read aloud each list. Play the game again using a new word ending.

Try It Out!

Make enough copies of the Try It Out! reproducible (page 27) to give half of the class a letter card and half of the class a word card. Cut apart the cards and distribute them. Remind students that they can add sounds to words to make new words. Sometimes the new words will be nonsense words, and sometimes they will be real words. Have each student holding a letter card pair with a student holding a word card. Direct students to try the letter sounds in front of the words.

Students should read their letters and words aloud to their partners but not show the cards to their partners. Help pairs try to blend sounds and words together to make new words. Encourage pairs to share the new words with the class and identify whether the words are real or nonsense. Then, have students change partners and try different sound and word combinations.

This Is the End

Because students often have an easier time adding word beginnings, spend extra time adding word endings. Play an alphabet game by having students go through the alphabet to find ending sounds that will create new words. Begin by saying, "The word is *bun*." Call on the first student to add the short /a/ sound to the end of the word to make *buna*. Ask students, "Is this a real word?" Students should say that it is a nonsense word. Repeat with the long /a/ sound, then move to /b/. Continue going through the alphabet, letting different students add sounds to the end of the word *bun*. Write real words on the board, such as *bunk*, *buns*, and *bunt*. Repeat with other words, such as *bee* (*bead*, *beef*, *beak*, *beam*, *bean*, *beep*, and *beet*), *say* (*safe*, *sage*, *sake*, *sale/sail*, *same*, *sane*, and *save*), *me* (*meek*, *meal*, *mean*, and *meat*), etc. Remember that the point is to make words with sounds, not just with the correct letters.

Try It Out!

Cut apart the cards. Try
different letters in front of the words.

b	b	race	race
t	t	ride	ride
p	p	rain	rain
d	d	rip	rip
g	g	rim	rim

Substitute Sounds

Ask, "What is a substitute teacher?" After several responses, explain that a substitute is another teacher who teaches a class when the usual teacher is absent. So, one teacher goes out and another comes in. Explain that substituting can also be done with sounds. Say, "Let's do a substitution for the word *can*. Take out the /n/ sound and put the /t/ sound in its place. What is the new word?" Students should say, "cat." Continue by saying, "We can also do a substitution with the new word *cat*. Take out the /t/ sound and put the /p/ sound in its place. What is the new word?" Students should say, "cap." Give students more practice substituting sounds by calling three students to the front of the class and having them stand in a row. Assign the /h/ sound to the first student, the short /i/ sound to the second student, and the /m/ sound to the third student. Have each student say his sound in turn. Have the three students repeat their sounds in turn again, this time a little more quickly. Do this again, until the three sounds blend together to make the word *him*. Then, make a substitution. Have the third student sit down and replace him with another student. Tell the third student to make the /l/ sound. Again, have each student say his sound until the sounds blend together to make the word—*hill*. Now, make another substitution. Ask the first student to sit down and have another student take his place. Tell this student to make the /w/ sound. Have students say their sounds and ask, "What is the new word?" Students should say, "will." Challenge students to come up with their own substitutions using the same process. Repeat until everyone has had a chance to say part of a word.

Abracadabra!

Explain that magicians have an old trick in which they put things in top hats, say "Abracadabra," and change the contents of the hats to other things. Tell students that they will be sound magicians and change words. Give each student a copy of the Abracadabra! reproducible (page 29). On the board, write the words *cat*, *bug*, and *pat*. Have each student choose one word and write it on the first hat on her reproducible. Then, ask each student to change the word into a new word by substituting one sound for another. For example, a student could change *cat* into *bat* by substituting the beginning sound. Or, she could change *bug* into *bag* by changing the middle sound. Or, she could change *pat* into *pad* by substituting the ending sound. Have each student write her new word on the second hat. Direct each student to draw pictures of the words in the boxes below the hats. Then, instruct students to cut out the hats and glue them back-to-back. Have students repeat with the boxes. Punch holes in the hats and boxes. Connect the hats and boxes by tying them together with string. Tie string through the top holes in the hats and hang them from the ceiling.

Abracadabra!

Choose one word from the board to change into another word. Write the word you choose on the first top hat and draw a picture of the word below the hat. Write the new word on the second hat and draw a picture of it below the hat.

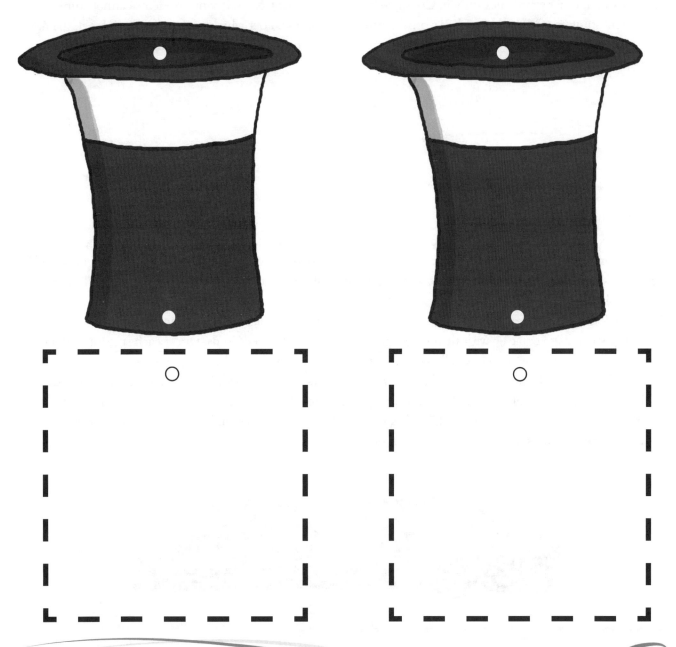

Strings of Substitutions

Remind students that they can substitute one sound in a word for another to create a new word. For example, *clip* becomes *click* when the ending /p/ sound is replaced with the /k/ sound. Some words can become several other words if different substitutions are made. On the board, model for students how the word *cat* can become *bat*, which can turn into *ban*, which can turn into *back*, which can then become *tack*, and finally *tuck*—simply by changing the first, middle, or last sound in each word. After this demonstration, give students a word and have them work together to make as many sound substitutions as possible to create only real words. (Nonsense words will not count.) Start with the word *ran*. Have a volunteer change one sound to make a new word and write the new word on the board. (Possibilities could be *run, rain, wren, tan, fan,* etc.) Say the new word so that students can think of another sound substitution. Continue building this string of words until students cannot think of another substitution. Count the total. Try other starter words and find out which one students can make the most substitutes for. Display that word with its record number of substitutions on the wall. Challenge students to break the record at later dates.

Riddle Book

Remind students that a word is made up of sounds and that they can create a new word by substituting one sound for another. Say to the class, "What do you get if you take *bug* and change the /b/ sound to the /m/ sound? "Students should answer *mug*. Ask, "What do you get if you take *dog* and change the /d/ sound to the /l/ sound?" Students should answer *log*. Explain to the class that these are sound riddles. Give each student a piece of paper. Write the following riddle-starter on the board: *What do you get when you take _____ and change _____ to _____?* Challenge students to come up with their own original words and changed words. Direct each student to write one riddle at the top of her paper and illustrate the initial word below the riddle. Then, have each student turn over her paper, write the answer, and illustrate it. If there is time, encourage students to write as many sound riddles as they can think of on separate sheets of paper. Assemble the pages into a class book. Add a construction paper cover with the title *Our Sound Riddles*. Read the book aloud and have students guess the answers to the riddles. Instruct students not to answer their own riddles!

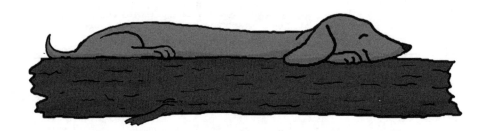

syl•la•ble

Multisyllabic Words

Introduction

After students feel comfortable working with phonemes, they will be ready to work with syllables. Syllable work helps students learn how to make long words manageable to spell and sound out while reading.

Duck, Duck, Syllable

Explain that in words, phonemes combine together to make up chunks of pronunciation called *syllables*. One way to understand syllables is to tap out the sounds. Model how to tap out syllables, starting with one-syllable words (*tea, play, boat, hat*) then moving to two-syllable words (*carrot, homework, action, friendly*), three-syllable words (*tomato, creative, musical, curious*) and four-syllable words (*disagreement, unimportant, Mississippi, responsible*). Tap the syllables lightly on a desk as you say the words and guide students to do the same. Have students play Duck, Duck, Syllable. Take students outside where they can run and have them sit in a circle. Choose one student to be "it" and have him stand outside the circle. Say a multisyllabic word. Have the student who is "it" walk around the circle and lightly tap a student's head for each syllable in the word. The student whose head is tapped on the last syllable should get up and chase "it" around the circle. If the student who is "it" races around the circle and sits in the chasing student's space before being tagged, the chaser becomes "it." If the chaser tags "it" before that student sits, he should return to his space. Give the student who is "it" a new multisyllabic word to tap out. Repeat until all students have had a chance to either be "it" or to chase "it" around the circle.

Teacher, May I?

Play a version of the Mother, May I? game. Explain that syllables are parts of words. Tell students that there are many ways to count syllables. One method is to clap each syllable while saying a word; another is to tap the syllables on a desk. A third way is for a student to place her hand just below her chin and say the word aloud. Each time her hand touches her chin, it counts as one syllable. Take students to a place outside where they can run. Assign students to five teams. Designate start and finish lines and have teams stand on the start line. Say a word to the first team from the word list below. Instruct team members to work together to count the syllables and say the answer, then tell them if they are correct. If the team is correct, have them take the same number of steps as the number of syllables in the word. If the team is incorrect, have them stay where they are. Repeat with the next team. The first team to cross the finish line wins.

Suggested words and numbers of syllables*:

report (2)	after (2)	people (2)
sunset (2)	sunshine (2)	employee (3)
happiness (3)	composer (3)	beautiful (3)
continue (3)	history (3)	candlestick (3)
applesauce (3)	professor (3)	president (3)
information (4)	impossible (4)	encouragement (4)
discovery (4)	interruption (4)	illustrator (4)
competition (4)	kindergarten (4)	

*Adjust number of syllables for regional pronunciations.

Syllable Bingo

Review the concept of counting syllables with students, then play Syllable Bingo. Give each student a copy of the Bingo Grid reproducible (page 33). Tell students to randomly fill the blank spaces with the numbers 1, 2, 3, or 4. Explain that these numbers correspond to the number of syllables in words they will hear. Randomly read words from the dictionary that have between one and four syllables. Each time you read a word, have each student silently count the number of syllables, then place a marker on each space on her card with a matching number. For example, if you read the word *pencil*, each student should count two syllables in the word *pencil* and place a marker on the space(s) with the number 2. Make a list of the words as you read them so that you will be able to check

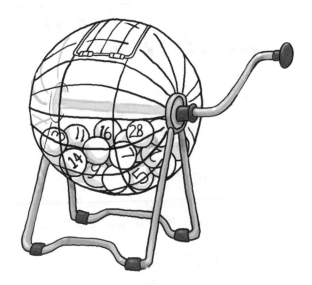

students' answers. Explain that the first student to get five markers in a row in any direction should say, "Bingo!" Check the student's answers, reward her if she is a winner, and continue the game until several more players win.

Syllable Math

In this activity, students will do math with words that have 4 or fewer syllables. Decide if you want them to add or multiply the numbers according to their math skill levels. For each problem on the Syllable Math reproducible (page 34), write either a plus sign or a multiplication sign to the left of the bottom square. Then, copy the reproducible for each student. Review how to count syllables in a word. Next, read each pair of words aloud or allow students to read them silently, and have them count the syllables silently. Tell students to write the number of syllables in the square next to each word. Then, have students either add or multiply the numbers. Review the answers with the class.

Addition Answer Key: 1. 6, 2. 7, 3. 5, 4. 5, 5. 7, 6. 4, 7. 7, 8. 6, 9. 4, 10. 7

Multiplication Answer Key: 1. 8, 2. 12, 3. 6, 4. 6, 5. 12, 6. 3, 7. 12, 8. 8, 9. 4, 10. 12

First-Rate Reading™:Phonemic Awareness and Phonics • CD-104019 • © Carson-Dellosa
Basics

Bingo Grid

Write the numbers 1, 2, 3, and 4
in the squares. Write only one number in each
square. Your teacher will explain how to play Syllable Bingo.

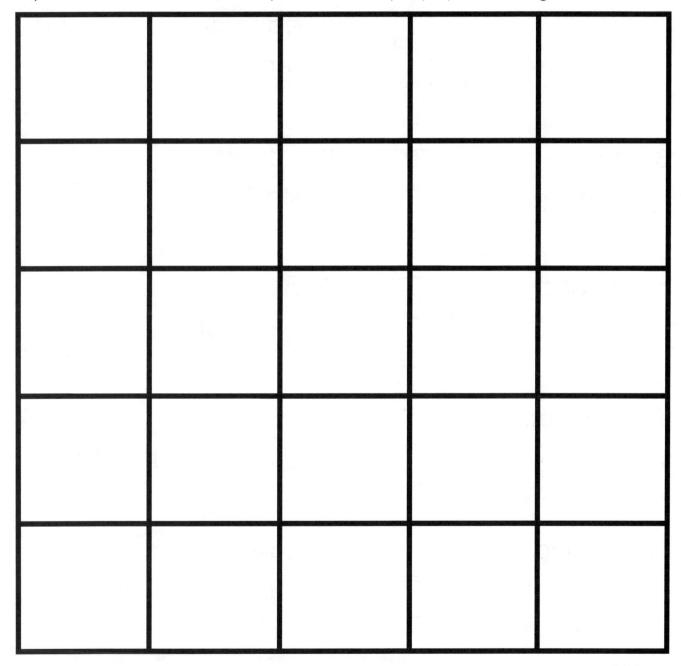

Syllable Math

Count the syllables in each word.
Write the number of syllables in the box next to the word. Do the math.

1. before
   overpower
   $\square$
   $\square$
   ___

2. education
   technical
   $\square$
   $\square$
   ___

3. referee
   meeting
   $\square$
   $\square$
   ___

4. rattlesnake
   starfish
   $\square$
   $\square$
   ___

5. anybody
   propeller
   $\square$
   $\square$
   ___

6. pride
   grasshopper
   $\square$
   $\square$
   ___

7. strawberry
   motorcycle
   $\square$
   $\square$
   ___

8. flower
   undefeated
   $\square$
   $\square$
   ___

9. clothing
   flashlight
   $\square$
   $\square$
   ___

10. unexpected
    hurricane
    $\square$
    $\square$
    ___

First-Rate Reading™:Phonemic Awareness and Phonics • CD-104019 • © Carson-Dellosa
Basics

Dictionary Keys

Give students keys to unlock the secret of new words. Remind students that a big word usually has more than one syllable. Explain that dictionaries are tools students can use to break big words into syllables. Give each student access to a dictionary and direct students to find the word *elephant*. Write *elephant* on the board. Explain that the dots, hyphens, or spaces in the word (depending on the dictionary) divide the word into syllables. For example, the word *elephant* is separated into three sections, which means that there are three syllables in the word. Tell students that a dictionary is key in learning a word's syllabication. Give each student two copies of the Dictionary Keys reproducible (page 36). Write the words *addition, calculator, challenge, jellyfish, tomorrow,* and *watermelon* on the board. Tell each student to use a dictionary to look up the words, then write each word under a key, showing how it should be divided into syllables. (The answers are *ad-di-tion, cal-cu-la-tor, chal-lenge, jel-ly-fish, to-mor-row,* and *wa-ter-mel-on*.) When each student finishes, have him cut out the keys and punch a hole in the top of each key. Have each student twist a chenille craft stick "key ring" through the holes to connect the keys. Hang the keys on a bulletin board titled "Keys to Finding Syllables." Use additional copies of the reproducible to have students look up other words.

Dictionary Race

Race through syllabication with this game. First, choose five or six multisyllabic words from the dictionary and write them on a piece of paper. Include the indicators that show the syllable breaks. Give each student access to a dictionary. Review how to find syllables in the dictionary, then direct students to look up the word *grandmother*. Write *grandmother* on the board. Ask a student to come up to the board and draw slashes where the syllable breaks would be (grand/moth/er). Repeat with additional words until students understand the concept. Next, have a dictionary race. Assign students to four teams. Have the teams form four lines facing the board. Write each team's name on the board. Tell each team to elect a team secretary who will write words on the board. Place a dictionary at the front of each line close to the board but not in students' hands. Spell (do not read) a multisyllabic word for both teams' secretaries to write on the board. When the secretaries step aside, say "Go!" Allow the first student in each team to race to a dictionary, look up the word to see how it is syllabicated, then draw slash marks between the syllables on the board. Give a point to the first student who correctly syllabicates the word. Have students decode the word by reading each syllable, then send the first student in each team to the end of the line. Ask the next team secretaries to erase the word, then spell a new word. Repeat the process until all students have been first in line. The team with the most points wins.

Dictionary Keys

Listen to the words your
teacher says. Find the words in a dictionary.
Write the words and syllable breaks on the lines
under the keys. Cut on the dashed lines.

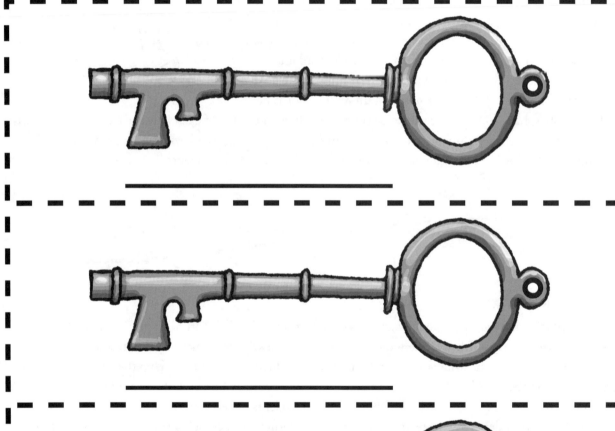

First-Rate Reading™: Phonemic Awareness and Phonics • CD-104019 • © Carson-Dellosa
Basics

Multisyllabic Cowboys

Explain that a big word usually has more than one syllable. One way to decode a multisyllabic word is to look for smaller, recognizable words in the big word. "Wrangle" some big words with this activity. Give each student two pieces of string, approximately 18" (about 46 cm) long; paper; and pencils. Direct students to write the word *cowboy*. Ask, "Do you see any smaller words in this big word?" After students find the words *cow* and *boy*, direct each student to use one piece of string to "lasso" (form a circle around) the word *cow* with the string. Then, have each student use his second lasso to make a circle around the word *boy*. Ask students to read the smaller words. Next, ask, "If you put these two smaller words together, what big word do you get?" After they tell you the answer, have students use the words *backyard*, *without*, *toenail*, *footstep*, and *birdhouse* to practice breaking multisyllabic words into smaller, decodable words. Have students write each word, then circle the smaller words with their strings. After reading each smaller word, have students put them together to form the bigger word.

The -Est Test

Explain that there are tricks to help students break down multisyllabic words. One trick is to look at the endings. Explain that if a word has *-ing*, *-er*, or *-est* added to the end, the ending usually counts as a syllable. If students cover up the ending, they can find the root word. If students learn to decode the root word and add the ending, they will be able to read bigger words. Because one of the endings is *-est*, call this activity the -Est Test. As an example, write the word *newest* on the board. Say, "Give it the -Est Test. Does this word end in *-ing*, *-er*, or *-est*?" After identifying the ending, have a student cover it with his hand. Ask the rest of the class, "What is the root word?" Students should be able to recognize the word *new*. Ask, "So, how would you say this bigger word?" Instruct students to add the ending to the root word to make the word *newest*. Have students use the -Est Test on additional words, such as *longest*, *meeting*, *taller*, *shortest*, *being*, *teacher*, *playing*, etc. When students are proficient at covering the word endings, allow them to practice covering prefixes in words, such as *reload*, *remake*, *unfriendly*, *unhappy*, *disappear*, *impossible*, *preview*, etc. Introduce these words by first teaching the words *pretest* and *retest* because students will recognize the word *test* from the -Est Test. Adjust the words to students' abilities and be sure to discuss the general meanings of these prefixes. Encourage students to use the -Est Test when they find multisyllabic words in their reading.

Syllable Puzzle

Remind students that multisyllabic words are words with many syllables. Review how to find the syllables in a dictionary by choosing several multisyllabic words. Have students look them up and put slash marks, dashes, or dots between the syllables to show where the syllables are. Then, have students make syllable puzzles. Give each student a sentence strip. Direct her to browse through a dictionary to find a multisyllabic word, then write it on her sentence strip. Next, tell students to make zigzag cuts between the syllables in the words. Have students mix up the puzzle pieces and trade puzzles with partners. Have each student reassemble her classmate's syllable puzzle and decode the multisyllabic word by reading each syllable. Tell students to use this strategy when they read independently. Give each student an envelope in which to store her syllable puzzle. Store the envelopes at a center for students to assemble during free time.

Syllable Concentration

As students become more familiar with the concept of multisyllabic words, let them practice counting syllables. Remind students of the different strategies for reading multisyllabic words (looking for smaller words inside a bigger word, doing the -Est Test by covering a suffix or prefix and then decoding the root, breaking a word into smaller syllables, etc.). Play a game using some of these strategies. Pair students and give each pair a copy of the Syllable Concentration reproducible (page 39). Tell students that there are four cards with two-syllable words, four cards with three-syllable words, and four cards with four-syllable words. Have each pair of students sit on the floor, cut apart the cards, mix them, and place them facedown in a grid arrangement. Tell one student to turn over two cards, read them, and count the syllables in the words. If the words have the same number of syllables, the student may keep the cards and take another turn. If the words do not have the same number of syllables, the student should turn over the cards and leave them in place, and the partner should take a turn. Remind students that there are four cards for each syllable amount, so there are two matches for each number. Have partners continue to play until all cards have been turned over. The student with the most cards wins.

Syllable Concentration

Cut apart the cards. Play
Syllable Concentration with a partner.

independent	working	understand
tallest	unfriendly	watermelon
sandpaper	sidewalk	supermarket
mailbox	stepladder	overpower

Syllable Sort

Gather a small box, a medium box, and a large box. (A small gift box, shoe box, and small appliance box would work.) Write *2* on the small box, *3* on the medium box, and *4* on the large box. Next, give each student three index cards. Remind students that words that have more than one syllable are called *multisyllabic words*. Review different strategies for reading multisyllabic words. Next, have students look around the classroom at posters, books, bulletin boards, etc., for multisyllabic words. Challenge each student to find one two-syllable word, one three-syllable word, and one four-syllable word. When students find their words, have them write the words on the index cards. Then, tell students to sort their words by placing the cards that have two-syllable words in the *2* box, three-syllable words in the *3* box, and four-syllable words in the *4* box. When students finish, remove the cards from each box, read the words, and ask the class to raise two, three, or four fingers to show the syllables. Either read the words in random order and re-sort them, or read them in order to check students' work. To make the activity more challenging, require students to make the words theme related. For example, have students search for science words, such as *larva*, *butterfly*, and *caterpillar*.

Syllable Charades

Use students' love for performing and moving to help them practice syllables. Write the following multisyllabic words on small pieces of paper: *handshake, footstep, horseshoe, rainbow, toothbrush, doghouse,* and *haircut*. If desired, choose curriculum-based words, as well. Teach students how to play a modified form of Charades. Have one student read a word to himself, then hold up his fingers to indicate how many syllables are in the word. Next, the student should silently help the rest of the class guess the word by acting out each syllable. He should hold up a finger to show which syllable he is acting out, then perform an action that helps his classmates guess the syllable's meaning when it is a word by itself. As the student acts out the syllable, classmates may raise their hands to guess. Call on students so that the performing student may remain silent. When all syllables have been identified, let classmates try to guess the entire multisyllabic word by helping them put together the syllables. Continue until each student gets a chance to perform.

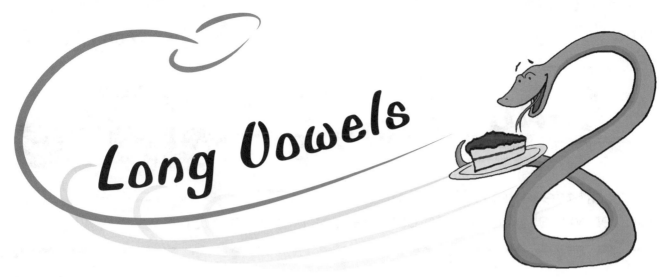

Long Vowels

Introduction

Use your knowledge of students' levels to assess whether they need to review short vowels and conduct reviews if necessary. (Refer to *First-Rate Reading™ Basics: Phonemic Awareness and Phonics, Grades 1-2* for short vowel activities.) Then, move into the more complicated realm of long vowels. Long vowels are more difficult because there are so many irregular ways to make vowels "say their names." Extra work in this area will prepare students to decode more complicated words.

Silent E Review

Review the sounds long vowels make or introduce them if necessary. Remind students that when a vowel sounds like its name, it is called a *long vowel*. Ask what long vowels students hear in the words *snake, weeds, mice, note,* and *universe*. Explain that there are many ways to make a long vowel sound. One way is to use a vowel-consonant-silent *e* pattern. Give each student a copy of the Long Vowels reproducible (page 42). Have students cut apart the letter cards and place the letters *a, t,* and *e* in front of them. Explain that when a word has a vowel-consonant-silent *e* ending, the first vowel usually says its name. Ask students to read the word *ate*. Next, have students place an *l* in front of *ate* and read the word *late*. Then, tell students to put a *p* in front of the word *late*. After students read the word *plate*, give each student a paper plate, and have her turn it over and write *plate* on the back. Instruct students to continue moving the letter cards around to create new words with the *a*-consonant-silent *e* pattern. Have students write the new words on the backs of the plates. Tell students that the letter *a* isn't the only vowel that uses this pattern—they all do. Instruct students to form the word *dine* with the letter cards. Ask them to decode the word, turn over their plates, and write *dine* on the fronts. Direct students to use their letter cards to form other *i*-consonant-silent *e* words to write on the plates. Finally, as a treat, provide small portions of cake and ice cream as a snack. (Get families' permission and check for food allergies and religious or other preferences before providing food.)

More Silent E Review

Continue working on long vowels made with silent *e*. Give each student a paper cutout of the letter *e*. Let students decorate their letters using markers, crayon, glitter, etc. Then, set a timer for two minutes. Let students walk around the room and look at posters, bulletin boards, etc., for consonant-vowel-consonant words that will use long vowels if a silent *e* is added. When students have created their words, call on each student one at a time to write the original word and the new word on the board and return to her seat. If you prefer not to have students move around the room to review silent *e* words, let them make lists of as many consonant-vowel-consonant words as possible. Then, have them create long vowel words by adding silent *e*'s where appropriate. Reward the student who lists the most correct words.

Name _____

Long Vowels

plate

Cut apart the letter cards. Your
teacher will tell you how to use the cards to form words.

a	b	c	d	e	e
f	g	h	i	j	k
l	m	n	o	p	q
r	s	t	u	v	w
x	y	z			

First-Rate Reading™:Phonemic Awareness and Phonics Basics • CD-104019 • © Carson-Dellosa

Vowel Team Review

Explain that there are many ways to make a long vowel sound. One way is to put two vowels side by side in a word to form a vowel team. Usually, the first vowel will "say its name" and the second vowel will be silent. Write the word *deal* on the board. Underline the *ea*. Explain that, "These two letters are vowels. The *e* says its name to make a long vowel sound and the second vowel is silent." Ask students to read the word *deal*. Tell students that this rule is usually true for all vowel teams, not just *ea*. Give each student a copy of the Long Vowels reproducible (page 42). Have students cut apart the letter cards. (Since the letter cards will be used with several other activities, consider having students save their letters in resealable, plastic bags.) Have students place the letters *b, e, a,* and *d* in front of them. Instruct students to use the vowel team rule to decode the word *bead*. On the board, write the word families *ead, eak, eal, eam, ean,* and *each*. Instruct students to place various consonants, blends, and digraphs at the beginning of the word families to create words. Next, give each student a copy of the Vowel Team Review reproducible (page 44). Have students write their *ea* words on the beads. Challenge students to use as many beads as possible. Then, tell students to cut out each bead and punch a hole in each end. Help each student thread string through each bead so that the end goes through the first hole of a paper bead, behind the word, through the second hole, and then through the first hole of the next bead. Have students wear their word beads for the rest of the day.

We All Scream for . . . Feet?

This sweet activity helps students differentiate between the *ea* vowel team and *ee* vowel combination. Give each student a piece of brown construction paper and a piece that is a different color, such as green, white, pink, etc. Have each student cut out a cone shape from the brown paper to resemble an ice cream cone and cut out two circles from the other color of paper. Have her glue the circles and cone together to look like a double scoop of ice cream. Next, have each student trace her feet on a sheet of white paper, cut out the feet, and tape them side by side. Randomly call out a list of *ee* and *ea* words, such as *bean, beef, cheat, cheer, cheese, cream, deep, fear, gear, geese, hear, heat, keep, leap, least, mean, near, neat, peach, peer, queen, seal, steer, street,* and *weed*. As you call out each word, instruct students to write it on the ice cream if the long /e/ sound is made with the vowel team *ea* or write it on the feet if the long /e/ sound is made with the vowel combination *ee*. Check students' answers when they finish. Consider writing words that are frequently misspelled on a word wall for future reference.

Vowel Team Review

Write *ea* words on the beads.
Cut them out. Punch holes in the small circles.
Thread a piece of yarn through the holes to make a necklace.

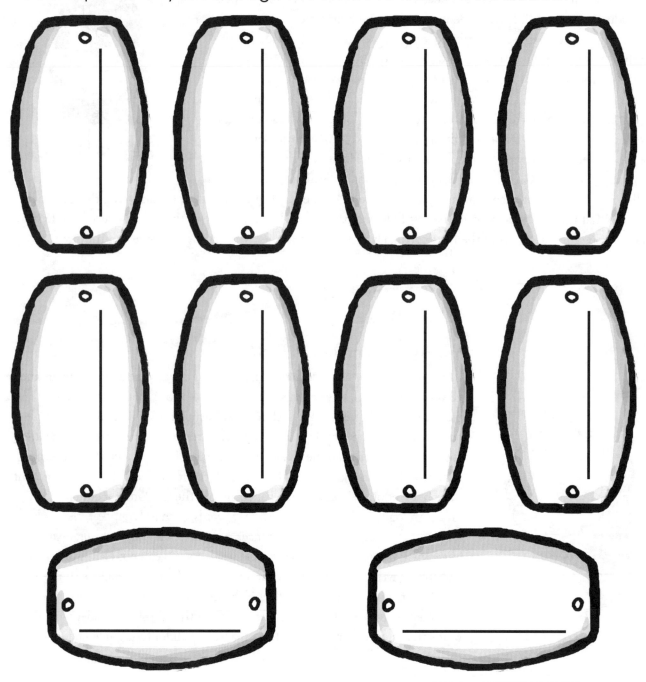

Calendar Days

Explain that there are many ways to arrange letters to make a long vowel sound. Remind students of the vowel team rule: when two vowels are next to each other in a word, the first sound usually "says its name" and the second vowel is silent. Or, use the saying, "When two vowels go walking, the first one does the talking." Remind students that sometimes the letter y also acts as a vowel. Write the word *may* on the board. Draw a line under the *ay*. Explain that when the letters *a* and *y* are together, they act like a vowel team. The first vowel, *a*, says its name, and the second vowel, *y*, is silent. Read the word *may* aloud, tracking the print with your finger as you read. Tell students that *a* and *y* in this word sounds like long /a/. Using the letter cards from the Long Vowels reproducible (page 42), tell students to find the letters *p, l, a,* and *y* and place the cards in front of them. Ask students to keep the *ay* rule in mind while sounding out the word *play*. Write the word *play* on the board. Encourage students to make other *ay* words by changing the beginning consonant(s). As students form words, list them on the board. After some time, give each student a copy of the Write It on the Calendar reproducible (page 46). Point out the *ay* in each day of the week. Then, explain that people write on calendars to remind themselves to do things on certain days. Tell students that they will use the *ay* words from the board to write sentences on the calendar. For example, they could use the word *play* to write the sentence *I will play with Susie* on the calendar. Other *ay* calendar words could include *day, May, today, yesterday,* etc., but students may use any *ay* word as long as it is used appropriately. Encourage students to write as many sentences as they can, then allow time for sharing.

Say What?

Explain that the letters *a* and *y* act like a vowel team. When *a* and *y* are together in a word, the first vowel, *a*, says its name, and the *y* is silent. Write the word *clay* on the board. Draw a line under the letters *ay*. Ask students to read the word. Repeat the word after them, tracking the print as you say each sound. Emphasize that the letters *ay* usually sound like long /a/. Give each student a large piece of construction paper. Using the letter cards from the Long Vowels reproducible (page 42), tell students to find the letters *s, a,* and *y*. Have students place the letters in front of them and decode the word *say*. Then, direct each student to draw a circle that takes up almost the entire piece of construction paper with a triangle in the lower corner to create a speech balloon. Tell each student to cut out the speech balloons and write the word *say* in it. Explain that cartoonists use speech balloons when characters have something to say. Explain that students will use the speech balloons to say other *ay* words. Have students spell other *ay* words with their letter cards. As students form the *ay* words, have them write the words in their speech balloons. Have students find partners. Have each student hold up his partner's speech balloon to look like the words are coming out of his own mouth. Let the partner read the *ay* words aloud. Then, ask students to switch roles. When students finish, staple the speech balloons to a bulletin board. Add the title "We're Talking about Long Vowels."

Write It on the Calendar

Write sentences
with *ay* words on the calendar.

Sunday	Monday	Tuesday	Wednesday	Thursday	Friday	Saturday

First-Rate Reading™: Phonemic Awareness and Phonics • CD-104019 • © Carson-Dellosa
Basics

When I Get Old

Explain that there are many ways to make a long vowel sound. Review some of the more common ways to make long vowel sounds. For example, remind students that if there is vowel-consonant-silent *e* in a word, as in the word *joke*, the vowel is long. Also remind them that if two vowels are together in a word, as in the word *boat*, the first vowel usually "does the talking" (says its name) while the second vowel "keeps walking" (is silent). Next, discuss yet another way to make a long vowel sound. Write the word *old* on the board. Tell the class that when the letters *o*, *l*, and *d* are together in a word, the /o/ sound is usually long. Say the word for students while tracking the print with your finger. Using the letter cards from the Long Vowels reproducible (page 42), tell students to place the letters *h*, *o*, *l*, and *d* in front of them. Have students read the word *hold* as you write it on the board. Guide students to form the words *told*, *sold*, *bold*, *cold*, *gold*, *fold*, *mold*, and *scold* with their letter cards. Have students read each word after forming it. Add each word to the list on the board. Then, have each student write a poem titled, "When I Get Old." Each student should write about what he thinks he will be like when he gets older. Direct students to use the *old* words from the board. When they finish, tell students to draw self-portraits that show what they will look like. Staple the pictures and poems to a bulletin board and add the title "When I Get Old."

New from Old

Remind students that long vowels can be made in various ways. Review the vowel-consonant-silent *e* pattern and the vowel team pattern. Then, tell students that the *o* makes the long sound when it is in front of the letters *l* and *d*. Using the letter cards from the Long Vowels reproducible (page 42), tell students to find the letters *g*, *o*, *l*, and *d*. Tell students to place the letter cards in front of them and read the word. Next, have students make gold coins out of *old* words. Give each student a piece of yellow construction paper. Have students draw or trace several circles that are large enough for students to write *old* words. Have students write the words *old* and *gold* in the circles. Guide students to add other consonants in front of the  letters *o*, *l*, and *d* to create new *old* words. Have students write these new words on the yellow circles, then cut out the circles. Give each student a piece of brown construction paper to decorate like an open treasure chest. Tell students to glue the yellow circles (or gold coins) inside the "treasure chests." Allow students to add gold glitter to their "coins," then add the title "My Vowel Collection." Reward students with chocolate coins covered with gold foil. (Before sharing food, get families' permission and inquire about food allergies and religious or other food preferences.)

Night Vowels

Explain that there are different ways to make the long /i/ sound. One way is to have an *i*-consonant-silent *e*. Explain that there is another way to make the long /i/ sound. Write the word *night* on the board. Underline the letters *-igh*. Tell the class that when the letters *igh* are together in a word they make the long /i/ sound. Say the word *night* as you track the print. Encourage students to make other *igh* words. Give each student a piece of white construction paper and a white crayon. Have them use pencils to lightly draw several horizontal lines on the paper, then have students write the word *night* on the first line. Using the letter cards from the Long Vowels reproducible (page 42), tell students to try different consonants in front of the *ight*. For example, tell students to try adding an *l* at the front of *ight*. Have students read the word *light*. When each student forms an *ight* word with her letter cards, have her use the crayon to write the

word on one of the pencil lines. Students may also add stars, moons, and even owls to their drawings using the white crayons. When students finish, have them use dark blue or black watercolors to paint over the crayon. Their words will magically appear in the night sky.

Igh Airlines

Introduce *igh* words with a high-flying activity. Explain that there is more than one way to make the long /i/ sound. Review the fact that when a word ends in *i*-consonant-silent *e*, the *i* makes a long vowel sound. Remind students that the letters *i*, *g*, and *h* also make the long /i/ sound. Write the word *flight* on the board. Draw a line under *igh*, then read the word to the class as you track the print. Next, write the word *high* on the board. Ask, "How would you read this word?" (Explain that this *high* means the opposite of low, not *hello*.) Give each student a piece of paper. Direct each student to write *flight* and *high* at the top of the paper. Using the letter cards from the Long Vowels reproducible (page 42), tell students to try different consonants and blends in front of the *igh* and *ight*. Have them write these new words on the paper. When students finish, distribute the Paper Airplane reproducible (page 49) and have them make paper airplanes. (Demonstrate this if necessary.) Say, "Since we have the words *flight* and *high* on this paper, we should make it into something that takes flight and goes very high!" Call on each student to say one of his long /i/ words and then sail his plane into the air.

Paper Airplane

Follow the directions
and drawings to make a paper airplane.

1. Place a sheet of paper word side
   up. Fold it in half, then unfold.

2. Fold corners A and B into
   the center of the paper.

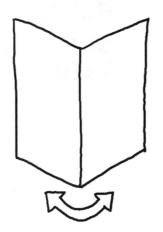

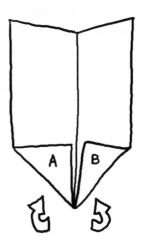

3. Fold corners
   C and D into
   the center of
   the paper.

4. Fold it in half
   again.

5. Fold down the
   wings evenly.

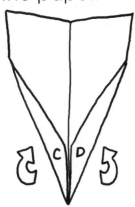

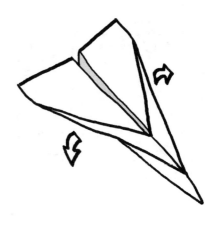

Word Window

Explain that there are many ways to make the long /o/ sound. Students should be familiar with the pattern *o*-consonant-silent *e*, as in the word *rope*, and with the vowel team *oa*, as in *coat*. Then, introduce another way to make the long /o/ sound—the *ow* combination. Write the word *window* on the board. Read the word to the class as you track the print. Give each student a copy of the Word Window reproducible (page 51) and a 3" x 5 $\frac{1}{2}$" (7.5 cm x 14 cm) piece of plastic wrap. Direct each student to cut out the letter cards and the panes of the window along the dashed lines. (Students may need help starting the window pane cuts.) Then, have students tape plastic wrap to the backs of their windows and place the letter cards behind the windows to make *ow* words. Work with students to decode each *ow* word as they make it. If students enjoy the activity, let them create additional letter cards to make other *ow* words. Supervise students so that the new letter cards will make long /o/ words.

Pillow Prompts

Teach a comfy way to make the long /o/ sound. Review the different ways to make the long /o/ sound. Remind students that one way is to put *o* and *w* together. Write the word *pillow* on the board. Tell students that in this word, *ow* makes the long /o/ sound. Give each student two pieces of white paper. Have students write the word *pillow* on one piece of paper. Using the letter cards from the Long Vowels reproducible (page 42), tell students to make the words *throw* and *below*. Tell students to write the words on both of their papers. For practice, have students form their own long /o/ words that end in *ow* and *own*. As each student forms words, have him add the words to both sheets of paper. When he finishes, let him place the two papers on top of each other with the blank sides together and glue around the edges of the paper, leaving one side open. Let the student stuff the "pillow" with scrap paper and close the last edge with glue. Let each student keep his pillow at his desk to study during quiet time.

Word Window

Cut out the letter cards and
window panes on the dashed lines.
Tape a piece of plastic wrap to the back of the window.
Place the letter cards behind the window to make *ow* words.

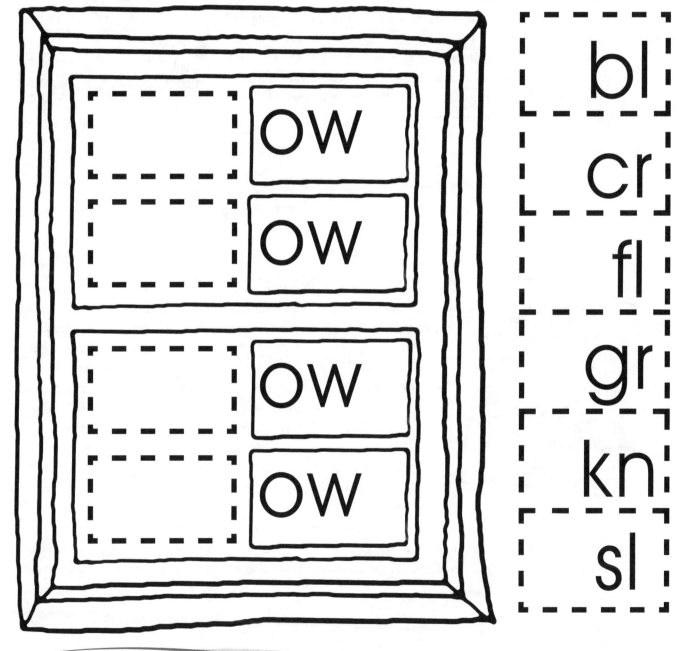

bl

cr

fl

gr

kn

sl

Plent-Y of Number Words

Explain that there are several ways to create the long /e/ sound. The letter combination *ee* and vowel team *ea* both make the long /e/ sound. Tell students that the letter *y* also makes the long /e/ sound in some words. Write the word *twenty* on the board. Explain that when the letter *y* is at the end of a two-syllable word, it is pronounced like a long /e/. Read the word *twenty* as you track the print. Write the number words *thirty, forty, fifty, sixty, seventy, eighty,* and *ninety* on the board. Work with students to decode each word. Then, challenge students by writing math problems on the board that have answers that end in *y*. Select operations depending on students' levels. For example, for second graders, use *10 + 10 = (twenty), 25 + 5 = (thirty), 50 - 10 = (forty),* etc. For third graders, use *5 x 4 = (twenty), 6 x 5 = (thirty), 5 x 8 = (forty),* etc. Arrange the problems so that the answers are not in numerical order. Direct students to copy the problems on paper, solve them, then write the number words for the answers. Review the answers with the class.

Party Letter

Review different ways to make the long /e/ sound, such as *ee* as in *feet* and *ea* as in *seat*. Then, look at another way to make the long /e/ sound—a *y* at the end of a two-syllable word. Have students use the letter cards from the Long Vowels reproducible (page 42) for this activity and give each student two index cards. Tell each student to write *l* and *z* on one card, and *n* and *p* on the other. Each letter should be as big as the letters on the reproducible. Have students cut apart the letters on the index cards and use all of the cards to form the words *party, chilly, candy, dirty, dizzy, family, funny,* and *happy*. After each word is formed, invite students to decode the words as you write them on the board. Next, instruct students to pretend that they just went to a great party and need to write thank-you notes. In the notes, students should describe favorite parts of the party to a friend who hosted it. Require students to use five of the words on the board and to draw lines under them as they use them. Model how to begin a friendly letter if necessary. When students finish, have them find partners and share their notes. Display the notes on a bulletin board covered with wrapping paper and decorated with balloons and streamers.

First-Rate Reading™: Phonemic Awareness and Phonics • CD-104019 • © Carson-Dellosa
Basics

Digraphs

Introduction

Digraphs are more difficult for students than blends because the letters make new and unexpected sounds. Use the following digraph activities as a review for students.

Sh Shop

Begin by explaining that when two letters are next to each other in a word and they make one sound, they are called a *digraph*. Write the word *shop* on the board. Draw a line under the letters *s* and *h*. Tell students that when *s* and *h* are next to each other, they make the /sh/ sound. Say, "It is almost like you are telling someone to be quiet—shhhhh." Have students make the sound after you and put their fingers to their lips. Read the word *shop* with students. Have students make other *sh* words. Give each student a copy of the Digraphs reproducible (page 54). Tell students to cut apart the letter cards. (Since these cards will be used with several activities, have students save them in resealable, plastic bags.) Let students make additional cards as needed or use letters from the Long Vowels reproducible (page 42). Direct students to find the letters *sh*, *a*, *k*, and *e* and place the letters in front of them. Work with students to decode the word *shake* as you write the word on the board. Guide students to make words like *shark*, *sheep*, *sheet*, *shelf*, *shell*, *ship*, and *shampoo* with their letter cards. After students have formed each word, add it to the list on the board. Then, help students open a *sh* shop. In the *sh* shop, only items that begin with the letters *s* and *h* will be sold. Give each student paper and crayons and let him choose four words from the list on the board. Have each student draw a picture of the item, write the word below it, and add a price tag. When students finish, collect the pictures. Create a display by grouping like items together. For example, if five students draw sharks, group the sharks together. Staple the pictures to a bulletin board as if they are on store shelves. Add the title "Our 'Sh' Shop."

Gone Fishin'

Fish for digraphs. Explain that when two letters next to each other in a word make one sound, they are called a *digraph*. One digraph is the *sh* combination. Write *sh* on the board and make the /sh/ sound for students to repeat. Explain that a digraph can be anywhere in a word. Write the word *fish* on the board. Draw a line under the *sh*, read the word, and track the print. Have students play Gone Fishin'. Pair students and give each pair a copy of the Gone Fishin' reproducible (page 55), a ruler, string, paper clips, tape, and a bar magnet. To make fishing poles, have each pair tie one end of the string to the ruler and tie the other end around a bar magnet. Have students cut out the fish on the reproducible, fasten a paper clip to each fish, and place the fish facedown on the floor. Let one student in each pair lower the magnet and try to "catch" a fish and read it. If the student reads it correctly, she should keep the fish. If she reads it incorrectly, she should place the fish facedown on the floor, and the next student may have a turn. The student with the most fish at the end of the game wins.

Name _____

Digraphs

Cut apart the letter cards.
Your teacher will tell you how to form words with the cards.

th	a	e	e	i	o
ch	o	<u>u</u>	<u>b</u>	c	<u>d</u>
kn	f	f	g	h	k
sh	l	l	m	<u>n</u>	<u>p</u>
ng	r	s	t	w	y

Name _____

Gone Fishin'

Cut on the dashed lines.
Use the cards with the Gone Fishin' game.

 blush

 cash

 dish

 fresh

 rush

 splash

 trash

 wish

 brush

Th Theater

Add a little digraph drama to students' routine. Write the letters *t* and *h* on the board. Tell students that when the letters *t* and *h* are together, they usually make the /th/ sound. (Note that you may have to explain the difference between "voiced" *th*, as in *then*, and unvoiced *th*, as in *theater*, if students notice the difference or if your phonics program calls for it.) Write the word *theater* on the board. Underline the *th*. Read the word for students to repeat as you track the print. Emphasize that *th* is one sound. Using the letter cards from the Digraphs reproducible (page 54), have students place the letters *th*, *i*, and *n* in front of them. Ask, "How would you read this word?" Encourage students to track the letters as they sound out the word. Write *thin* on the board. Guide students to form the words *thank, thick, thing, think, third, thirsty, three, throw,* and *thunder*. Write each word on the board after students read it. Then, ask, "Can you think of any other words that begin with the /th/ sound that are not on the list?" Add their suggestions to the board. If students cannot think of any, suggest *thief, thirty, thought, thorn,* and *thump*. Challenge students to write *th* tongue twisters using the words on the board. Give students an example, such as, "Thirty thieves thought thumps were thunder." Tell students that not every word has to begin with *th*, but the more *th* words they use, the better. Direct students to write down their tongue twisters. Explain that the *Th* Theater is very fancy, so students should try to read their tongue twisters with very clear pronunciation. Schedule time for all students to perform their *th* tongue twisters in the *Th* Theater. After all students have shared their tongue twisters, have students vote on the one that is most difficult and try to master it as a class.

Th Wreath

Give each student a large paper plate. Explain that when the letters *t* and *h* are next to each other, they make one sound. Say the /th/ sound for students to repeat. Tell students that this sound can come at the beginning, middle, or end of a word. Write the word *wreath* on the board. (Explain that the *w* is silent in this word.) Draw a line under the *th* in the word *wreath*. As you track the print, say the word for students to repeat. Have students use the letter cards from the Digraphs reproducible (page 54) to form the following *th* words: *bath, cloth, fourth, fifth, length, math, both, path, teeth,* and *with*. Write the words on the board. Next, have students make *th* wreaths. Show each student how to fold her paper plate in half and cut out the middle. Tell each student to choose at least six *th* words from the board, write them on construction paper, cut them out, and glue them to the back of the paper plate circle. Encourage students to add other decorations to their wreaths, such as glitter, ribbon, confetti, etc. Have students read their *th* words to the class, then hang the wreaths from the fronts of their desks as decorations.

Talented Chickens

Explain that when the letters *c* and *h* are next to each other in a word, they usually make one sound. Say the /ch/ sound for students to repeat. Write the word *chicken* on the board. Draw a line under the *ch* and read the word aloud as you track the print. Help students practice reading other *ch* words. Give each student several index cards. Write the word *chat* on the board for each student to copy on an index card. Ask, "How would you read this word?" Work with students to decode the *ch* word. Repeat the procedure with other *ch* words, such as *chose, chop, chip, chin, chime, children, chess, cheese,* and *check*. After reviewing the words, say, "Did you know that there are some talented chickens that can read words? You will meet some of them today." Give each student a lunch-sized paper bag and a copy of the Talented Chickens reproducible (page 58). Have students cut out the puppet pieces and glue them to their bags. Show students how to place their hands in the bags and pretend that the chicken puppets are picking up items with their "beaks." Assign students to small groups. Have one student in each group place her *ch* word cards facedown on the floor. Have group members take turns using their chicken puppets to pick up cards. After a chicken picks up a card, have the student read the *ch* word. Tell students to take turns until there are no more cards.

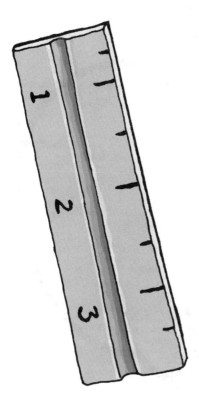

Inch by Inch

Review the fact that when *c* is next to *h* in a word, it makes one sound. Say the /ch/ sound and have students repeat it. Tell students that the /ch/ sound can come at the beginning, middle, or end of a word. Write the word *inch* on the board and read it aloud as you track the print. (If your students use metrics, explain that an *inch* is a unit of measurement equal to 2.54 cm.) Ask a volunteer to underline the two letters that make the /ch/ sound. Have students use their letter cards from the Digraphs reproducible (page 54) and place the letters *m, u,* and *ch* in front of them. Invite students to read the word *much* as you write it on the board. Guide students to form and read the following *ch* words: *such, lunch, bunch, rich, reach, beach, each, peach, bench,* and *branch*. Add each *ch* word to the board. Next, give each student a piece of paper and a ruler. Direct students to trace the shape of the ruler on the paper and cut it out. Have students make little marks to indicate inch lines. Then, direct each student to write *inch* at the beginning of the ruler. Have each student choose three more *ch* words from the board and write them on her paper ruler. Pair students and have them read their *ch* words to each other. Create a display by stapling the paper rulers end to end. Add the title "Our 'Ch' Words Measure Up!"

Talented Chickens

Color and cut out the puppet pieces. Glue them to a paper bag to make a chicken puppet. Use the puppet to help you work with *ch* words.

Word Wheel

Some phonics programs teach the *wh* digraph as a /wh/ sound while others teach it as the /w/ sound. Decide how to teach this activity and the following one based on the preferences of your phonics program and adjust the activity according to whether the digraph includes the /h/ sound. Write the letters *w* and *h* on the board. Explain that when the letters *w* and *h* are together at the beginning of a word, they make one sound. Make the sound for students. Write *wheel* on the board. Have students use the letter cards from the Digraphs reproducible (page 54) to form the words *whale, wheat, while, whimper, whine, whirl, whisker, whisper,* and *white*. Have students read each word as you add it to the board. Next, give each student a copy of the Word Wheel reproducible (page 60). Explain that the picture is a wheel. Have each student choose eight *wh* words from the board, write one word on each spoke of the wheel, then cut out the wheel. Next, have each student practice reading the words to a partner. Finally, let each student punch a hole in the middle of her wheel and thread a piece of string through it, then spin (or whirl) the wheel on the string.

Interview

Explain that the letters *w* and *h* form one sound. Make the sound for students to repeat. Explain that many question words start with *wh*. Write *what* on the board for students to read. Say, "You may use this word at the beginning of a question, such as *What is your favorite TV show?*" Add the words *when, where,* and *why* to the board for students to read. Let volunteers give sample questions using each word. Explain that these words are often used to interview people, then have students conduct their own interviews. Pair students and have each student write four interview questions for his partner that begin with the *wh* words *what, when, where,* and *why*. When students

finish, have them use the questions to interview their partners. Direct Partner A to ask Partner B one question. Have Partner A write down the answer. Then, have partners switch roles until all questions have been answered. Have each pair share one question and answer with the whole class.

The King of Digraphs

Write *king* on the board. Draw a line under the letters *n* and *g*. Explain that when these two letters are together, they usually produce one sound. Read the word aloud and track the print. Let students use the letter cards from the Digraphs reproducible (page 54) to make as many *ng* words as possible and have them write the real words they make on pieces of paper. Have students start with *ing* by adding different consonants to the beginning. Repeat with *ong* and *ang*. For extra incentive, tell students that the student with the most *ng* words will be crowned "King (or Queen) of the Digraphs."

Word Wheel

Write *wh* words on the spokes
of the wheel. Cut out the wheel.

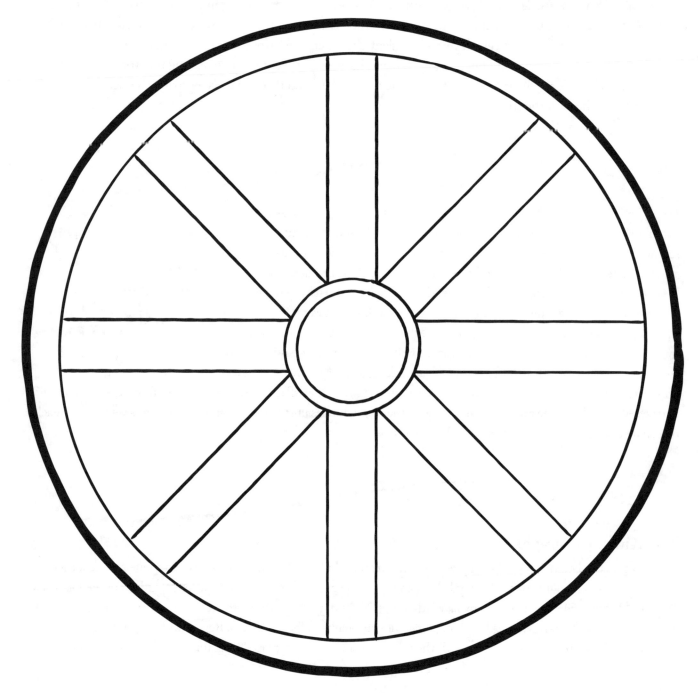

First-Rate Reading™:Phonemic Awareness and Phonics • CD-104019 • © Carson-Dellosa
Basics

Ring Finger

Explain that when the letters *n* and *g* are next to each other, they usually make one sound instead of the individual /n/ and /g/ sounds. Write the word *ring* on the board. Draw a line under the letters *n* and *g* and say the word for students. Have students use their letter cards from the Digraphs reproducible (page 54) to place the letters *f, i, ng, e,* and *r* in front of them. Help students decode the word. Also, have students form *ring, strong, wing, thing, young, long, bang, hang,* and *hunger.* Have students decode these as you write them on the board. For additional practice, give each student a piece of paper. Have her trace her hand on the paper and cut it out. Have each student draw a ring on one finger and write the word *ring* on that finger. Tell each student to choose four other *ng* words from the board to write on the remaining four fingers. Have students color their hands, then have each student read her *ng* words aloud to a partner. Create a display by stapling the paper hands to a bulletin board. Add the title "Let's Give 'Ng' Words a Big Hand!" Reward students with small, plastic rings to wear or let them make their own rings from chenille craft sticks.

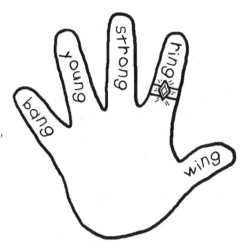

Tie the Knot

Increase students' knowledge of the digraph *kn.* Explain that when the letters *k* and *n* are together in a word, they usually make the /n/ sound. Write *knot* on the board. Underline the *kn.* Read the word for students. Explain that this knot is the kind they get in their shoelaces. It is different than the word *not.* Have students use their letter cards from the Digraphs reproducible (page 54) to form the words *knife, kneel, knit, knob, knock, know,* and *knuckle.* Have students decode each word as you write it on the board. Next, give each student five index cards. Have each student choose five words from the board to write on her index cards. Direct her to punch a hole in the top of each card, loop yarn through the holes, and tie knots with the yarn. Let students take turns reading their words aloud. To review the words, hang a piece of rope in the classroom. Use the words as the week's vocabulary by letting each student spell the words orally to you. As each student completes his spelling assignment, let the student tie a knot in the rope. When all students have spelled the words, display a sign over the rope labeled "Our Knots Mean Knowledge!"

Knee Slapper

Explain that when the letters *k* and *n* are next to each other in a word, they usually make the /n/ sound. Write the word *knee* on the board. Draw a line under the letters *kn*. Ask, "How would you read this word?" Using their letter cards from the Digraphs reproducible (page 54), have students place the letters *kn*, *e*, and *e* in front of them. Help students decode the word *knee*. Instruct students to form the following *kn* words: *knew, kneel, knead,* and *knight.* Then, say a list of words that includes words that begin with /n/, such as *knew, nest, knight, nine, name, kneel,* or *noise.* If students think that the word begins with the *kn* digraph, have them slap their knees lightly. If the word does not begin with *kn,* students should do nothing. As students slap their knees to the correct words, write the words on the board.

Graphing Digraphs

Use a little math to teach the *ph* digraph. Write the following words on index cards: *phase, phone, photo, phrase, phony, Phil, phonics, dolphin, nephew, sphere, graph, Joseph, triumph, paragraph.* Next, write the words *beginning, middle,* and *end* at the bottom of a piece of bulletin board paper. Explain that when the letters *p* and *h* are together in a word, they usually make the /f/ sound. The digraph *ph* can be at the beginning, middle, or end of a word. Write the word *graph* on the board. Ask students to read the word. Then, have the class sort and graph some *ph* words. Give half of the students cards with *ph* words and instruct them to try to read their words to the class. Have remaining students decide if the *ph* is at the beginning, middle, or end of each word. After each word is read and voted on, let a volunteer tape the word card to the appropriate column of the graph. When there are no more index cards, let students call out their own words. Write these words on cards and graph them if they contain the *ph* digraph.

Variant Vowels

Introduction

Variant vowels, also called r-controlled and l-controlled vowels, are vowels whose sounds are changed because they are next to the letters *r* or *l*. Depending on your phonics program, explain that the letter *r* next to a vowel often makes the /er/ sound, or the /schwa + r/ sound. Also explain that the letter *l* next to a vowel often makes a /schwa + l/ sound. Although students usually have trouble because the vowels do not make their normal sounds, the words are easy to recognize because of the letters *r* and *l*.

Ir Garden

Let students "get a little dirt on their shirts" and see if they can hear the rhyme in two words. Write the words *dirt* and *shirt* on the board. Draw a line under the letters *i* and *r*. Say each word as you track the print. Ask, "What sound did the letters *i* and *r* make in the word *dirt*?" Have students form other *ir* words with the /er/ sound. Give each student a copy of the Variant Vowels reproducible (page 64). (Since students will be using the letter cards in several activities, have them save the letters in resealable, plastic bags.) Have students cut apart the letter cards and place the letters *s* and *ir* in front of them. Ask students to read the word, then write it on the board. Work with students to form the words *stir, shirt, skirt, squirt, birthday,* and *girl*. Have students read each word as you write it on the board. Then, give each student four craft sticks and a disposable cup filled with dirt. Direct her to write the word *dirt* on one end of a craft stick. Let each student choose three more *ir* words from the board to write on the craft sticks. Tell students to write *ir* and their names on the cups. Explain that sometimes gardeners label their plants with signs pushed into the earth. Have students push their craft sticks into the dirt to identify their *ir* words, then water the dirt. Secretly add a few small flower seeds to each cup. Place the cups in a tray on a sunny windowsill and let students water them every few days until the plants sprout.

Bird Word

Move from the ground (dirt) to the sky (birds) with *ir* lessons. Write the word *bird* on the board. Explain that the letters *i* and *r* make an /er/ sound. Read the word *bird* aloud. Using the letter cards from the Variant Vowels reproducible (page 64), have students place the letters *b, ir,* and *d* in front of them. Review the sound with the class. Ask, "How do we read this word?" Have students take away the *b* and replace it with *t* and *h*. Have students read *third* as you write it on the board. Repeat by replacing the *d* in *third* with the letters *s* and *t*. After students read the word *thirst*, write it on the board. Repeat with the words *first, fir, stir, swirl,* and *twirl*. Next, give each student a copy of the Bird Word reproducible (page 65). Tell each student to write the word *bird* on the bird, color it, and cut it out. Then, give each student a sentence strip. Have students choose several *ir* words (other than *bird*) from the board and write them on the sentence strips. Have each student glue the bird's feet to the top of the sentence strip. Staple several sentence strips end to end to look like birds sitting on a telephone wire. Make several rows if necessary. Say a list of *ir* words but mix in other words with different vowel sounds. When students hear the variant vowel combination *ir*, have them chirp like birds.

Variant Vowels

dirt

Cut apart the letter cards.
Your teacher will tell you
what words to make with the cards.

all	a	b	c	d
ar	f	g	h	j
aw	k	l	m	n
ir	p	r	s	t
or	t	w	qu	y

First-Rate Reading™: Phonemic Awareness and Phonics • CD-104019 • © Carson-Dellosa

Basics

Name _____

Bird Word

Color and cut out the bird.
Glue the bird's feet to a sentence strip.

"Hare"-pin Turn

Try this "hare"-raising variant vowel lesson. Write *hare* on the board. Underline the *are*. Explain that when the letters *are* are together in a word, they usually sound like /air/. Have students read the word *hare*. Tell students that a *hare* is a rabbit, and the kind of hair on your head is spelled differently. Give each student a copy of the "Hare"-pin Turn reproducible (page 67) and a paper fastener. Have each student cut out the hare, the letter wheel, and the window on the hare. Tell each student to place the wheel behind the hare, push the paper fastener through the dot on both patterns, and spread out the fastener on the back of the wheel. Have each student turn the wheel so that the *h* is showing in front of the *are*. Ask students to read the word again, then tell them to turn their letter wheels so that the *c* is showing. Have students read *care*. Continue having students turn the letter wheel and read the other words. Direct each student to write a sentence for each word. Finally, reward students with hare food: carrot sticks! (Before completing any food activity, ask families' permission and inquire about students' food allergies and religious or other preferences.)

Pick Up *Are* Words

Write the word *square* on the board. Underline the letters *are*. Explain that these letters make an /air/ sound. Read the word for students. Then, write the word *dare* on the board. Ask, "If *s, q, u, a, r, e* sounds like *square*, what do you think *d, a, r, e* sounds like?" Continue with additional words, such as *mare, care, fare, hare, rare, blare, scare, share, spare,* and *stare*. Next, assign students to groups of four. Give each group 12 craft sticks. Direct group members to work together to write the *are* words on the craft sticks. Then, instruct students in each group to gather the sticks and drop them. Have students take turns picking up the sticks. Player A in each group should try to pick up a stick without moving any other sticks. If Player A moves another stick, he loses his turn. If Player A picks up the stick successfully, he must read the word on the stick correctly to keep the stick and let the next student have a turn. If Player A reads the word incorrectly, he should replace the stick in the pile and let the next student have a turn. Warn students that sometimes no one can pick up a stick without moving another stick. If that happens, the group members can agree to re-drop the remaining sticks. The first player in each group to get four sticks and form a square is the winner.

Superstars

Give each student a piece of yellow paper. On the board, model how to draw a star and help each student draw a star on his paper that is large enough for him to write a word inside each point. (Provide a pattern if needed.) Write *star* on the board. Draw a line under the letters *a* and *r*. Explain that the letters *a* and *r* make an /ar/ sound. Have students repeat the word as you track the print. Have each student write *star* in the middle of his paper star. Next, have students use their letter cards from the Variant Vowels reproducible (page 64) to place the letters *c* and *ar* in front of them and read the word *car*. Have students make more words by adding letters in front of *ar* and adding letters to the end, as well. As students form other words, direct them to write the words on the points of their stars. Have students cut out the completed stars. Create a display by stapling the stars to a black background. Add the title "SuperstARs." Let each student attach a few star stickers to the display for extra sparkle.

"Hare"-Pin Turn

Cut out the hare and the letter wheel. Cut out the square on the hare. Push a paper fastener through the dot on each piece. Turn the letter wheel to form new *are* words.

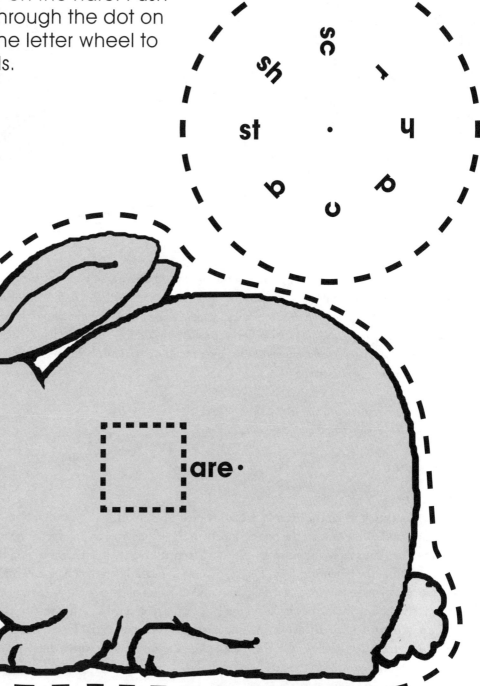

The *Ar* Farm

Explain that the letters *ar* make an /ar/ sound. Write the word *farm* on the board. Ask students to decode the word, then have students form other *ar* words. Write the phonograms *arm*, *ard*, *ark*, and *art* on the board. Direct students to use the letter cards from the Variant Vowels reproducible (page 64) to add different consonants and blends to the beginning of each phonogram. Have students write any words they form on pieces of paper. Next, write the song lyrics below on the board. Sing the song to the tune of "Old MacDonald Had a Farm." Have students suggest *ar* words from their lists. Write the word in the spaces. Then, have students read and sing the song with you. Repeat as often as desired with other *ar* words.

Old MacDonald had a farm, a, r, a, r, /ar/,
And on this farm he had a _____, a, r, a, r, /ar/,
With a _____, _____ here and a _____ , _____ there,
Here a _____, there a _____, everywhere a _____, _____,
Old MacDonald had a farm, a, r, a, r, /ar/.

Quick Draw

Explain that when the letters *a* and *w* are together in a word, they usually sound like a short /o/ (or make a similar sound, depending on your phonics program). Write *draw* on the board. Underline the letters *a* and *w*. Work with students to decode the word *draw*. Give students paper. Write one of the following words on the board: *claw, saw, jaw, paw, straw, crawl, lawn, yawn,* or *fawn.* When you say, "Quick draw!" have students silently decode the word, then draw quick pictures of it. After a few minutes of drawing time, have students hold up their pictures. Do a quick assessment, give the answer, then go on to the next word.

Paw Prints

Remind students that when the letters *a* and *w* are next to each other in a word, they usually make the short /o/ sound or a similar sound. Write *paw* on the board, underline the letters *a* and *w*, and read the word aloud. Give each student a copy of the Paw Prints reproducible (page 69). Have students use their letter cards from the Variant Vowels reproducible (page 64) and find the letters *p* and *aw*. Direct students to place different consonants and blends in front of the phonogram *aw* to make *jaw, law, raw, flaw, slaw,* and *straw.* Challenge students to form other words with *awl* and *awn.* Tell them to write any words they make on the Paw Prints reproducible. After writing the words, let students lightly color the paw prints and cut them out. Let students share their *aw* words. Tape the paw prints to the floor to make animal tracks. Each day, at the end of the tracks, place a sentence strip with a different *aw* word written on it. Allow students to follow the tracks to the new word each day.

Paw Prints

Write *aw* words on the paw prints.
Cut out the paw prints.

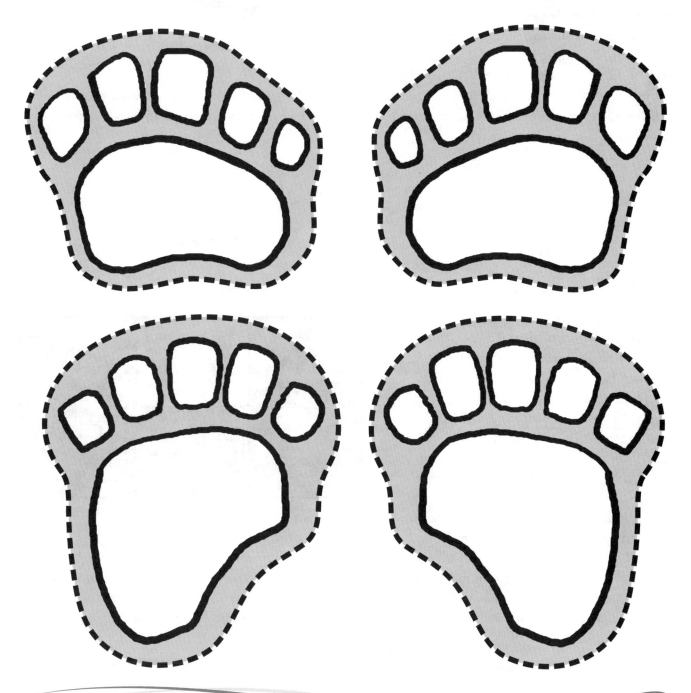

Have a Ball

Explain that when the letters *a*, *l*, and *l* are next to each other in a word, the *a* sounds like a short /o/ sound (or similar sound, depending on your phonics program). Write *all* on the board. Read it aloud and say a sentence with the word, such as "I want *all* of the doughnuts." Write *ball* on the board. Ask, "Is *a*, *l*, *l* in this word? What sound does the *a* make?" Next, have students sit on the floor in a circle. Roll a ball to one student. When the student catches the ball, say an *all* word, such as *call, tall, wall, small, fall, hall, mall*, or *stall*, for the student to spell. If the student spells

the word correctly, she should roll the ball to another student. If she spells the word incorrectly, ask classmates to help her, then have her roll the ball to another student. Continue having students spell words and keep the ball rolling to maintain students' interest.

Small Mall in the Hall

Continue work with *all* by explaining that the sound of the letter *a* changes if it is next to *ll* in a word. Write *mall* on the board and read it to the class. Have students use their letter cards from the Variant Vowels reproducible (page 64) to place different consonants and blends in front of the letters *all*. As students form words, have them raise their hands. Call on students to write their words on the board. Next, have students make a small mall in the hall. Give each student a piece of drawing paper. Ask, "What do you see when you go to a mall?"

Remind students that stores in a mall sell many different products and that mall stores have storefronts. Instruct each student to draw a storefront using one of the *all* words from the board. For example, a student could draw a store that sells balls, a store named Call Me that sells phones, etc. Encourage students to be as creative as possible. Post the store pictures on the wall in the hallway, inviting other classes to "shop." Add the title "Thank You for Visiting Our Small Mall!"

Fork It Over

Explain that when the letters *o* and *r* are next to each other in a word, they usually sound like /or/. Write *fork* on the board and underline the *or*. Sound out the word. Have students use their letter cards from the Variant Vowels reproducible (page 64) to place the letters *or* and *k* in front of them. Guide students to form different *or* words by placing *c*, *p*, and *st* in front of *ork*. Have each student write *cork*, *pork*, and *stork* on a piece of paper. Next, write *orn*, *ort*, and *ord* on the board. Let students try adding different consonants and blends in front of each, and write down any *or* words they build. Finally, give each student a plastic fork and a paper plate or bowl, and tell him to spread out his *or* words in front of him. Read a list of random words, including some words from the *or* lists. When students hear the *or* words, they should use their forks to lift the paper words onto their plates. Check to see that students lifted all of the same words onto their plates. Celebrate the /or/ sound with a class snack of popcorn! (Get families' permission and check for food allergies and religious and other preferences before serving food.)

Storming the Fort

Continue working with the letters *o* and *r*. Write *fort* on the board. Read the word aloud and explain that a *fort* is a building made to resist attacks. Write *storm* on the board and have students read it as you track the print. Explain that *storm* can be a weather term, but it can also mean to go in a group to attack. Have students play a game called Storming the Fort. Divide the class into two large groups. Tell students that they are in "forts." Write the phonograms *orch*, *ord*, *ork*, *orm*, *orn*, and *ort* on the board. Instruct each group to use their letter cards from the Variant Vowels reproducible (page 64) to cooperatively form as many different *or* words as possible by adding different consonants and blends in front of the *or*. Designate group members to record each word. After 10 minutes, tell one group to read one *or* word. Write the word on the board. Then, let the other fort respond with one of their *or* words. Continue until one team runs out of words. The team that has the most *or* words without repeating any of the words has "stormed the fort."

Diphthongs

Introduction

Diphthongs are perhaps the most difficult phonics concept to pin down simply because there are so many ways to say words with diphthongs. Also, phonics programs use a wide variety of methods to teach them, and dictionaries use many different tricks to show how they should be pronounced. Use the following activities to fine-tune students' skills in this area.

Word Coil

Begin teaching the difficult concept of the *oi* diphthong by explaining that when *o* and *i* are next to each other in a word, they sound like /oy/ as in *foil*. (Pronunciations will vary widely due to regional dialects.) Have students repeat the sound. Write *oil* on the board and underline the *oi*. Read the word aloud as you track the print. Give each student a copy of the Diphthongs reproducible (page 73) and the Word Coil reproducible (page 74). Direct students to cut apart the letter cards on the Diphthongs reproducible and place the letters *c*, *oi*, and *l* in front of them. (Since students will be using these letter cards with several activities, have them save the letters in resealable, plastic bags.) Work with students to decode the word *coil*. Ask, "What is a coil?" Show an example by having students look at the Word Coil reproducible. Next, have students add other consonants and blends in front of the phonogram *oil*. When a student forms a word, have him write it on the coil on the Word Coil reproducible. After writing several words, pair students and have them read *oi* words together. Then, have the class cut out the coils. Give each student a piece of string and tape. Tell students to tape the string to the x. Play with the coils and introduce onomatopoeia by discussing the different sounds coiled springs make (*boing* and *sproing*). Point out the *oi* in each word.

Foiled Again!

Explain again that when *o* and *i* are next to each other in a word, they make the /oy/ sound. Write *foil* on the board. Read the word aloud as you track the print. Ask, "Which two letters in this word made the /oy/ sound?" Next, have students use letter cards from the Diphthongs reproducible (page 73) and place the letters *f*, *oi*, and *l* in front of them. Challenge students to take out the *f* and try different consonants and blends at the beginning of *oil*, as well as other phonograms, such as *oin* as in *coin* and *join* and *oint* as in *joint* and *point*. Give each student a piece of paper on which to write *oi*, then have each student write at least four *oi* words and cut them out. Provide aluminum foil, construction paper, and glue for each student. Tell each student to glue the letters *oi* in the middle of the foil, then glue the *oi* words around the *oi* on the foil. Glue the foil to construction paper frames and staple the sheets to a bulletin board. Add the title "Our 'Oi' Words Shine!"

Name _____

Diphthongs

Cut apart the letter cards.
Your teacher will tell you how to use them to form words.

oi	**ou**	**ow**	**oy**
b	**c**	**d**	**e**
f	**g**	**h**	**j**
l	**a**	**n**	**p**
r	**s**	**t**	**v**

Word Coil

Write *oi* words on the coil.
Cut it out. Tape a piece of string to the x.

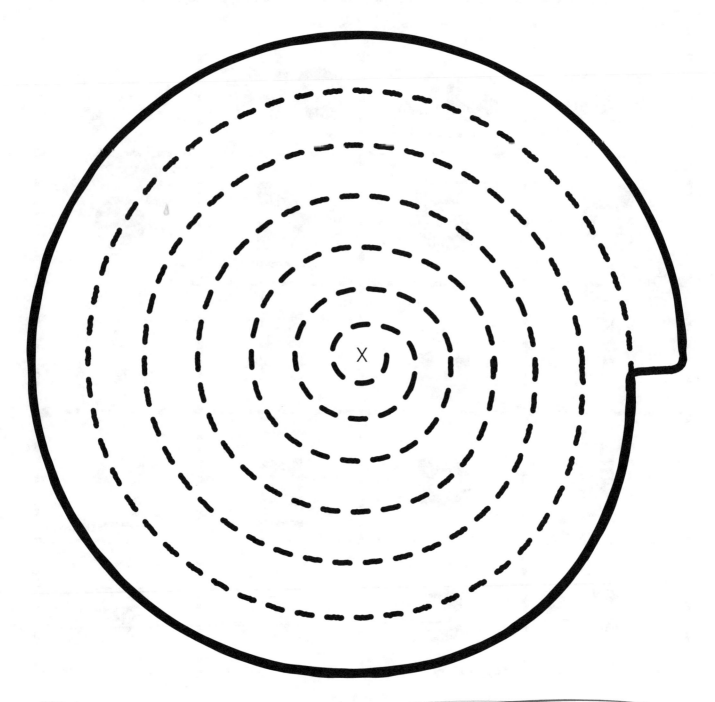

X

That's the Point

Explain again that when the letters *o* and *i* are next to each other in a word, they sound like /oy/ as in *coin*. Write *coin* on the board for students to decode. Have students use the letter cards from the Diphthongs reproducible (page 73) to put the letters *c, oi,* and *n* in front of them. After reading the word, have students try adding other consonants and blends in front of the phonogram *oin*. Write their words on the board. Challenge students to create other *oin* words, such as *join, joint,* and *point*. After forming the word *point*, tell students that they will point out other *oi* words. Give each student a piece of paper, a pencil, a ruler, and tape. Direct each student to point her index finger and raise her thumb, then place her pointing hand on the paper to trace. Have each student cut out her pointing hand and tape it to the top of a ruler, orienting it so that the pointing finger is like an extension of the ruler. Finally, have students search for *oi* words in books, on posters, and on bulletin boards. When students find words, tell them to use their paper hands to point to the words. Call on various students to read their *oi* words.

Enjoy the Toys

Explain that there is more than one way to make the /oy/ sound. Another way to make the /oy/ sound is with the letters *o* and *y*. Write *toy* on the board and read it as you track the print. Ask, "What two letters in this word make the /oy/ sound?" Have students use their letter cards from the Diphthongs reproducible (page 73) and place the letters *b* and *oy,* in front of them as they sound out the word. Write *boy* on the board. Repeat to form the following *oy* words: *cowboy, joy, ploy, Roy, royal, loyal, destroy, decoy,* and *voyage*. Next, have students use some of these words to design toys. Give each student a piece of drawing paper. Tell each student to choose one or two *oy* words from the board and design a toy that is somehow related one of the words. For example, a student could draw a toy ship that goes on a voyage, a jack-in-the-box that brings people joy, or a toy cowboy. Encourage students to be creative as they draw, color, and write descriptions about their toys (including how they are related to *oy* words). Tell the class to underline the *oy* words they use. After students finish, allow them to read their toy descriptions aloud. Place strips of brown paper on a bulletin board to look like shelves and staple the toys above them. Add the title "Enjoy Our Toys."

Riddle Me This

Continue working with the *oy* diphthong. Have students use the letter cards from the Diphthongs reproducible (page 73) and place the *oy* cards in front of them. Read aloud the *oy* word riddles below. Explain that all answers will have *oy* in them. Encourage students to use the cards to spell the answers. Write each correct answer on the board.

Word Riddles

1. This word means extreme happiness, has one syllable, and starts with the /j/ sound. (*joy*)
2. This word means to bother someone. It has two syllables. The first syllable is *an*. (*annoy*)
3. This is a boy's name that begins with the /r/ sound and has *oy* in it. (*Roy*)
4. This is something fun to play with. It has one syllable. It starts with the /t/ sound. (*toy*)
5. This person may raise and rope cattle for a living. *Cow* is the first syllable. (*cowboy*)

Oy Decoy

Write the following /oy/ "words" on index cards: *boy, coyn, oyl, toy, joy, loyal, poynt, enjoy, soyl, destroy,* and *voyage.* Tape the words to a piece of chart paper. Write *decoy* on the board. Explain that some people make wooden *decoy* (pretend) ducks that can float in ponds. A person can even buy an instrument to make a wooden duck sound like it is quacking. But, no matter how much the decoy looks and sounds like a duck, it isn't! Have students look for decoy words. Remind students that the vowel teams *oi* and *oy* both make the /oy/ sound. Show students the words on the index cards and say that some of them are *oy* decoys. They look like and sound like *oy* words, but they are not. Point to *boy* and ask if students think that is the real spelling or a decoy. Reveal that it is the real spelling and leave the card on the chart paper. Move to the word *coyn* and ask, "Do you think this is the real way to spell *coin,* or is this a decoy?" Reveal that the word is a decoy and remove the card from the chart paper. Continue with the remaining words. Post the chart paper for reference.

Cloudy Words

Explain that when the letters *o* and *u* are next to each other in a word, they make the /ow/ sound as in the word *cloud.* Write *cloud* on the board and read it aloud as you track the print. Also stress that you are reading *aloud* and add that word to the board. Give each student two pieces of white construction paper. Have each student draw the outline of a simple cloud on one piece of paper, place the cloud paper on top of the blank paper, and cut out two clouds. Have each student write *ou* in the middle of one cloud. Using the letter cards from the Diphthongs reproducible (page 73), let students form *ou* words, such as *cloud, loud, proud, pound, round, found, sound,* and *ground.* Have each student read each word, then have him write the *ou* words on one of his cloud papers. When students have decoded and written the words, instruct them to make clouds with the papers by placing the two matching cloud pieces on top of each other so that the words face out. Have each student staple the edges of the clouds, leaving a small opening on one side, and stuff scrap paper or cotton balls inside to make the cloud puffy. Attach the clouds to a bulletin board covered with blue paper and titled "We're on Cloud Nine with 'Ou' Words."

Kangaroo Pouch

Continue working with the *ou* diphthong. Write *pouch* on the board for students to decode. Explain that a *pouch* is a pocket. Explain that mother kangaroos carry their joeys (babies) in their *pouches,* so have students carry *ou* words in pouches. Give each student an envelope and a piece of paper. Have students use the letter cards from the Diphthongs reproducible (page 73) to place the letters *p, ou, c,* and *h* in front of them. Then, have students write *pouch* on the fronts of their "pouches" (envelopes). Let students form other *ou* words using the phonograms *ouch, ound,* and *ouse* by placing different consonants, blends, and digraphs in front. When students form real words, ask them to write the words on the paper. After students finish brainstorming, have them cut apart the words and place the words in their "pouches." Have students pretend to be kangaroos by bouncing around, meeting with classmates, taking words from their pouches, then bouncing off to find other partners.

Ou Hounds

Release the *ou* words! Write the word *hound* on the board. Draw a line under the letters *o* and *u*, read the word aloud, and explain that bloodhounds are excellent trackers. They can use their sense of smell to find lost people. Many of these dogs serve on search and rescue teams. Let students be *ou* hounds. Explain that their job is to track down words that have the letters *o* and *u* in them and make the /ow/ sound. Assign students to three large groups. Tell one group that they will track three-letter *ou* words. Encourage students to look in books, dictionaries, and posters for the words. When the group finds a three-letter *ou* word, have them write the word on a piece of paper. Tell the second group that they should look for four-letter *ou* words and have the third group look for five-letter *ou* words. When students complete their research, gather the class together. Have the three-letter group read the

words they found as you record them on a piece of chart paper. Repeat with the four-letter group and the five-letter group. Review the words with the class and eliminate any that do not make the /ow/ sound. Which length of *ou* words is the most common? Close the lesson by asking students, "What is one sound that *ou* makes?"

How Now, Brown Cow?

Explain there are at least two ways to pronounce the letters *ow*. One way to say them is like the long /o/ sound, as in the word *snow*. Another way to say them is like the /ow/ sound, as in the word *cow*. Write *cow* on the board and read it for students. Have students use their letter cards from the Diphthongs reproducible (page 73), find the letters *c* and *ow*, and place them on their desks. Give each student a copy of the How Now, Brown Cow? reproducible (page 78). Explain that the cow on the reproducible has blank spots. Let students work with their letter cards to form new *ow* words. When a student finds a word, tell him to write it on one of the cow's spots. Next, write the following phonograms on the board: *ow*, *owl*, and *own*. Instruct students to try adding different consonants, blends, and digraphs in front of the phonograms to form words, such as *now*, *how*, *growl*, *prowl*, *down*, *town*, and *brown*. Have students write the words on the cows' spots, cut out the cows, and color them brown. Display the cows on a bulletin board covered with large spots of black and white paper, or with green grass and a fence. Add the title "Have You HERD Our 'Ow' Words?"

Celebrate by having some brown cow juice: chocolate milk! (Get families' permission and check for food allergies and religious and other preferences before serving food to students.)

How Now, Brown Cow?

Write *ow* words on the cow.
Cut out the cow and color it brown.

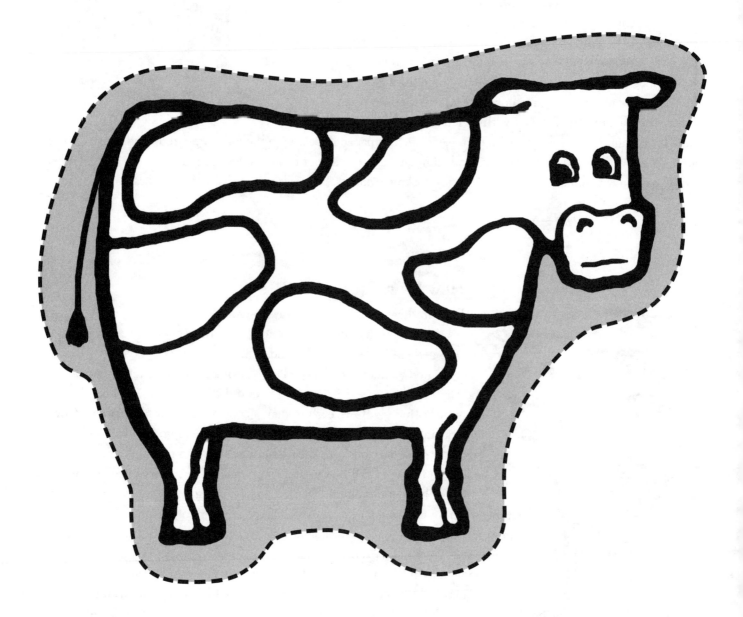

Towel Rack

Explain that *ow* has at least two sounds. One common sound is long /o/ as in *row*. Another sound is /ow/ as in *now*. Give each student a light-colored piece of construction paper. Using their letter cards from the Diphthongs reproducible (page 73), have students find the letters *t, ow, e,* and *l* and place the letters in front of them. Work with students to decode the word *towel*. Explain that sometimes people monogram towels to personalize them. Write the phonograms *ow, owl,* and *own* on the board. Instruct students to try adding different consonants, blends, and digraphs in front of the

phonograms. When students form recognizable words, have them personalize "towels" by writing the words on the construction paper. Challenge each student to write at least five words. Then, have students cut fringe at the tops and bottoms of their construction paper. Have students practice reading their *ow* words to each other. For extra fun, let students bring in towels from home and spend a few minutes lounging on them during story time. Read a story that contains some *ow* words, such as *Click, Clack, Moo: Cows That Type* by Doreen Cronin (Simon and Schuster, 2000).

I Crown Thee

Remind students of the two different ways to pronounce the letters *o* and *w*. Using their letter cards from the Diphthongs reproducible (page 73), have students place the letters *c, r, ow,* and *n* in front of them and decode the word. Give each student a copy of the I Crown Thee reproducible (page 80). Direct students to form as many *ow* words as they can and write the words on their reproducible crowns. Suggest that students try adding different consonants, blends, and digraphs to the beginning of the phonograms *ow, owl,* and *own*. When students finish, tell them to cut out and decorate their crowns with crayons, markers, and glitter. Tape each crown to a sentence strip, then tape each student's crown around her head. Have students walk around the classroom and "bow down" to each other's *ow* words.

I Crown Thee

Write *ow* words on the crown.
Cut out the crown. Tape it to a sentence strip. Tape the ends
of the sentence strip together to make the crown fit your head.

First-Rate Reading™:Phonemic Awareness and Phonics • CD-104019 • © Carson-Dellosa
Basics